FABULOUS
FELT
CRAFTS

50 CREATIVE
& COLORFUL
PROJECTS
TO MAKE

Katherine Duncan

LARK BOOKS
A DIVISION OF STERLING PUBLISHING CO., INC.
NEW YORK

ACKNOWLEDGEMENTS

Thanks to the real "authors" of this book—the thirty fabulous designers who lent their time, energy, and enthusiasm to create the imaginative projects that compose this book.

Congratulations to art director Dana Irwin for her continuing great eye for photo styling, to photographer Evan Bracken for his patience and accomodation through the many steps of a photo shoot, and to art director Celia Naranjo for her characteristically clean, balanced, and inventive layout.

Many thanks to Kunin Felt and National Nonwovens for their donations of felt for the projects, as well as Therm O Web and Beacon Chemicals for their donations of adhesives.

Good thoughts to the polite men and women who answered the phone at Foam and Fabrics in Asheville when I had yet another sewing question to ask. And thanks to Waechter's Silk Shop in Asheville who so willingly lent us samples of ribbons, buttons, and threads for the photo shoot.

Photography Styling and Design:
Dana Irwin
Page Design and Production:
Celia Naranjo
Photography:
Evan Bracken
Assistant Editor:
Heather Smith
Production Assistant:
Hannes Charen
Models:
Cindy Burda, p. 48
Claire Solomon, pps. 69, 72, 73
Sarah Hutchinson, p. 39

Daffodils on p. 5 created
 by Terry Albright.
Stocking on p. 6 created
 by Nancy Magaha.
Wall hanging on p. 7
 created by Dana Irwin.
Mosaic bottle on p. 7
 created by Barbara
 Matthiessen.

Library of Congress Cataloging-in-Publication Data

Duncan, Katherine.
    Fabulous felt crafts : festive projects for you to make/Katherine Duncan.—1st ed.
        p. cm.
    Includes index.
    ISBN 1-57990-156-5 (paper)
        1. Felt work. I. Title.

TT880 .D76 2000
746'.0463—dc21   99-054242

10 9 8 7 6 5 4 3 2 1

First Edition

Published by Lark Books, a division of
Sterling Publishing Co., Inc.
387 Park Avenue South, New York, N.Y. 10016

© 2000 by Katherine Duncan

Distributed in Canada by Sterling Publishing,
c/o Canadian Manda Group, One Atlantic Ave., Suite 105, Toronto, Ontario, Canada M6K 3E7

Distributed in Australia by Capricorn Link (Australia) Pty Ltd., P.O. Box 6651, Baulkham Hills,
Business Centre, NSW 2153, Australia

If you have questions or comments about this book, please contact:
Lark Books
50 College St.
Asheville, NC 28801
(828) 253-0467

Produced by Asia Pacific Offset, Printed in China

Contents

Introduction

My childhood memories of felt include bright red Christmas stockings laden with an assortment of decorations such as glitter, rickrack braid, and yarn. Around the Christmas tree was a precious and worn felt skirt adorned with cotton-stuffed appliqués. Sequins, some of them dangling on old, loose threads, simulated shining ornaments.

Every year, it was ceremonial to take out the stockings and tree skirt from their musty box, unfold them, and revel in the swirl of escaping glitter that heralded the beginning of the season. These holiday accoutrements grew better with age.

Parents and their children still make and cherish things made of felt. Traditionally, felt was made from compressed wool. Today, there are many varieties of commerically made felt on the market, many of which are made from synthetic fibers that can be washed. Some of these felts are embossed with richly textured designs that simulate snakeskin, leather, or wallpaper. Others have a soft, plush surface. In addition, the palette of colors available is almost unlimited. Commercially made wool felts are still just as popular as ever. Purists claim that there is nothing like the feel of wool felt, which has a heavier weight and smoother texture than synthetic felts.

Whatever your preferences, you're sure to find them among the projects in this book. From an antique white, bound-to-be-an-heirloom table runner with silk embroidery, to a kitschy, pink cocktail skirt with appliqués, there is a range of ideas and materials for every taste and level of ability.

Many of the projects involve simple sewing; many use only glue or other easy adhesives for attaching pieces of felt together. Almost all of the projects can be simplified, if needed, or made more complex. (If you don't want to sew on appliqués, for instance, you can glue them on. Or, if you aren't satisfied with a surface decorated with glued-on pieces of felt, you can add sewn-on embellishments such as beads, buttons, and sequins.)

The contributions to this book are made by a host of creative designers—some of them are full-time artists, but the majority of them are people with other careers. Those designers who had never worked with felt before were delighted with the ease with which their ideas translated into this forgiving fabric.

Dana Irwin imagined a 19th-century painting translated into a wall hanging composed of felt brushstrokes for a

6

child's room (page 28), Barbara Matthiessen envisioned a bottle covered with tiny pieces of randomly cut felt mosaics to hold fresh-cut flowers (page 84), and Terry Albright dreamed of perpetually fresh, felt daffodils to cheer up her winter windowsill (page 74).

Straight from the imaginations of these clever designers, you'll find exciting projects to choose from on the following pages which make great gifts, contribute to the beauty of your home, or enliven your wardrobe. We even included a couple for your dog or cat! Some of the projects are easy enough for your kids to make, while others will satisfy the most avid sewer.

Choose your favorites, make them, learn from your experience, and, eventually, you'll find yourself designing your own fabulous felt crafts!

Materials and Tools

Felt is one of the most compliant of fabrics. It doesn't unravel when you cut it, readily accepts the pierce of a sewing needle, lies flat where you place it, and doesn't slip or slide.

Felt is easy to cut, glue, and sew with basic, inexpensive tools. You'll find all the supplies that you need for felt crafts at your favorite fabric or craft store. The tools that are listed for each of the projects in this book are easy-to-find items such as scissors, rotary cutters and mats, and various types of sewing and embroidery needles.

You can buy a variety of felts at most fabric stores, but it's wise to call and ask about the store's selection before driving a long distance. If you can't find certain felts that you want to use, such as the harder-to-find embossed felts, you can order them by using the information on page 128. Most companies will send you a brochure with felt samples, which allows you to order your choices over the phone or via the internet.

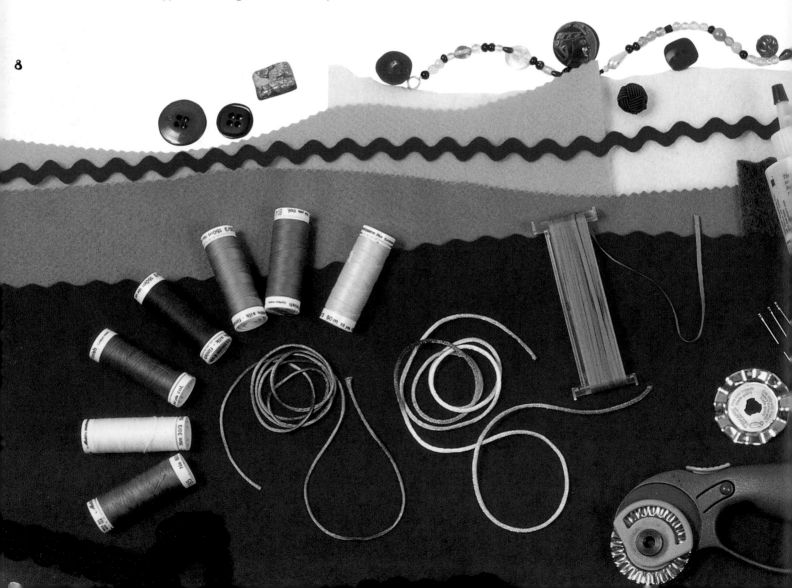

To Sew or Not to Sew?

If you don't sew, there are several adhesives available that are easier than ever to use. (Follow the manufacturer's directions when using them.) Fast-drying fabric glue works well on felt because it doesn't tend to soak the surface and leave blots like standard white glue. (If you choose to use this glue, make sure that you work in a well-ventilated area; the fumes are strong.) If you use white glue, which is a better choice for small children, use a paintbrush to spread a thin, even layer of glue onto the felt. Allow white glue to dry overnight once you've assembled the piece.

Double-sided sheets of adhesive are fun and simple to use if you're attaching felt cutouts to another surface, whether fabric, glass, or wood. To use this product, simply peel off one of the two paper backings, stick felt on it, trace your pattern in reverse on the other paper-covered side, and cut out the piece with scissors.

Fusible web, which has been around for years and saved many a torn hem at the last minute, can effectively be applied to felt. Iron-on adhesive is just as easy to use. Both are available in paper-backed sheets to protect your iron from getting gunked up when you apply the web or adhesive to the felt. First, iron the paper side of the web or adhesive onto a sheet of felt, trace your pattern in reverse on the paper side, and cut out your design.

Then, when you're ready to apply the piece, peel away the remaining paper backing, and stick it onto your surface.

Then peel away the paper, and iron the piece right side up onto your felt base.

Fun Felt Projects

Thumb through the following pages full of color, style, and creative verve to find your favorite felt projects. Read through the instructions before deciding if a project is right for you, and then begin to gather your materials. If you want to tailor a project to your own tastes by changing the colors, don't hold back—imagination is a powerful force! Ready, set, GO!

Bold Geometrics

Brightly colored felt pieces are skillfully combined to make the unusual projects in this section—our designers discovered that they could transform any surface with felt!

Great Garb

Felt isn't just for fedoras! From jewelry to purses, felt can be made into smashing accessories.

Fun Stuff

You don't have to be a kid to appreciate the zany, wonderful creations in this section!

Flowers and More

Cheer up your home, even in the darkest months, with the simple beauty of flowers.

Lasting Treasures

Create keepsakes that celebrate your connections with family or tradition.

Playing Card Coasters

Dress up a card game with these smart-looking coasters that your buddies will appreciate. Don't forget the peanuts!

You Will Need

- 9 × 12-inch (22.5 × 30 cm) felt pieces in the following colors: 2 black, 1 white, and 1 red
- 9 × 12-inch (22.5 × 30 cm) sheet of plastic canvas
- 1 skein white cotton embroidery floss
- 1 skein red cotton embroidery floss
- Scissors
- Chalk marker
- Embroidery needle
- Fabric glue

Instructions

1. Enlarge the patterns on page 115 to the size indicated, and cut out the shapes.

2. Cut eight pieces out of the black felt, each 4 inches (10 cm) square. Cut four pieces from the white felt, each 3 inches (7.5 cm) square.

3. Use the chalk marker to trace one spade and one club onto the black felt. Cut the shapes out. Trace the heart and diamond patterns once onto the red felt, and cut the shapes out.

4. Cut four, 3½-inch (8.8 cm) squares from the sheet of plastic canvas.

5. Squeeze fabric glue onto the back of each of the shapes, and then press them into place in the center of the white squares. Thread a needle with three strands of red embroidery floss, and blanket-stitch (see page 114) around each shape after it's in place.

6. Center each of these four units on a black square. Glue them in place, and allow them to dry. Thread the needle with three strands of red floss, and blanket-stitch around each white square.

7. Thread the needle with three strands of white floss. Blanket-stitch each of the four layered pieces to a black square on three sides. Before sewing up the last side, sandwich a square of plastic canvas between the two pieces of black felt. Stitch up the remaining side.

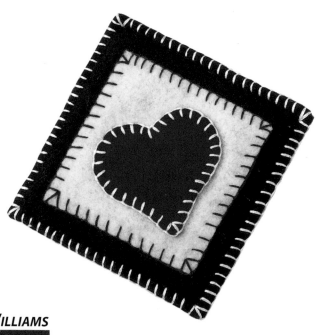

DESIGNED BY
CAROLYNN WILLIAMS

Felt Cards

These unusual cards optimize color and geometry. With some simple stitches, scissors, and glue, you can create your own.

DESIGNED BY
TERRY TAYLOR

You Will Need for All Cards

- Metallic embroidery/blending thread
- Blank cards and envelopes
- Wax paper
- Craft or fabric glue
- Scissors
- Scalloped-edge craft scissors
- Tapestry needle
- Straight pins
- Heavy book or weight

BURGUNDY SQUARES

You Will Need

- 2 x 3½-inch (5 x 8.8 cm) rectangle of green felt cut with scalloped-edge craft scissors
- 2 rectangles of burgundy felt cut with plain scissors, each 1¼ x 1⅜ inches (3.1 x 3.4 cm)

Instructions

1. Pin the burgundy felt rectangles inside the green felt rectangle with straight pins, leaving an even border around them.

2. Thread the tapestry needle with metallic thread.

3. Sew a large cross-stitch (see page 114) in the center of both burgundy pieces, and tie each off at the back of the piece.

4. Sew ¼-inch (6 mm) straight stitches around the perimeter of each burgundy rectangle to hold it in place.

5. Use small dots of glue to secure the felt to the card. Cover the card with wax paper topped with a weight to dry.

PINK BARS ON LIME GREEN
You Will Need

- 2 × 4-inch (5 × 10 cm) rectangle of lime green felt cut with scalloped edge
- 3 pink felt rectangles cut with scalloped edge, each ½ × 1½ inches (1.3 × 3.8 cm)
- Scrap of pink felt
- Hole punch
- Piece of typing paper

Instructions

1. To make cleanly cut pink felt circles, place a sheet of typing paper behind the scrap of pink felt. Place both layers in the hole punch and squeeze out four pink dots.

2. Space the pink felt rectangles on top of the green felt, leaving an even border around their perimeters. Secure them with straight pins.

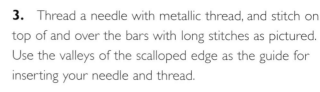

3. Thread a needle with metallic thread, and stitch on top of and over the bars with long stitches as pictured. Use the valleys of the scalloped edge as the guide for inserting your needle and thread.

4. Position the pink dots between the pink rectangles. Use a single stitch in the center of each dot to secure them to the background.

5. Use small dots of white glue to secure the felt to the card. Cover with wax paper, and weigh down with a book to dry.

HOT PINK AND BLUE TIC-TAC-TOE
You Will Need

- 2½-inch (6.25 cm) square of blue felt cut with scalloped edge
- 2 inch (5 cm) square of pink felt cut with scalloped edge
- Fabric marker or pen

Instructions

1. Use a fabric marker or pen to sketch a tic-tac-toe grid filled with Xs on the pink square of felt. Center the pink felt square on the blue square, and pin in place with straight pins.

2. Thread a needle with metallic thread. Use long stitches to create the lines of the tic-tac-toe grid. Stitch over the Xs with small cross-stitches.

3. Attach the felt to the card with glue, and allow it to dry.

GREEN SQUARE AND YELLOW CIRCLE

You Will Need

■ 2½-inch (6.25 cm) square of dark green felt cut with scalloped edge

■ ¾-inch-diameter (1.9 cm) circle of dark green felt

■ 2-inch-diameter (5 cm) circle of yellow felt cut with scalloped edge

■ Scrap of paper

■ Hole punch

Instructions

1. Position the scrap of paper behind the green felt circle, and cut a hole in the center with the hole punch.

2. Position the green circle on top of the yellow circle. Thread a needle with metallic thread, and sew it in place with four straight stitches radiating from the punched center.

3. Place a large scrap of paper behind the yellow circle, and use a hole punch to cut eight evenly spaced holes around the circumference of the circle.

4. Thread a needle with metallic thread, and use short, straight stitches placed equidistantly between the punched holes to secure the yellow circle to the green felt square.

5. Attach the felt to the card with glue, and allow it to dry.

16

YELLOW AND BLUE RECTANGLES

You Will Need

▪ 2 x 4-inch (5 x 10 cm) rectangle of bright yellow felt cut with scalloped edge

▪ 1½ x 3¼-inch (3.8 x 8.1 cm) rectangle of navy blue felt cut with scalloped edge

▪ Scrap of paper

▪ Hole punch

Instructions

1. Place a scrap piece of paper behind the blue rectangle. Punch eight evenly spaced holes about ½ inch (1.3 cm) from the edges.

2. Pin the blue shape to the bright yellow shape.

3. Thread a needle with metallic thread, and make long cross-stitches (see page 114) that form Xs between the punched holes.

4. Attach the felt to the card with glue, and allow it to dry.

GREEN AND HOT PINK DIAMOND SHAPE

You Will Need

▪ 2¼-inch (1.1 cm) square of green felt with scalloped edge

▪ 2-inch (5 cm) square of hot pink felt with scalloped edge

▪ Scrap of paper

▪ Hole punch

Instructions

1. Place a piece of paper behind the hot pink square and make evenly spaced holes with a hole punch around the edge of the square. (Begin at the four corners, then add the holes between.)

2. Center the pink square on top of the green one, and pin it in place.

3. Thread a needle with metallic thread, and make straight stitches through the outside edge of each hole to the edge of the pink felt.

4. Visually extend the lines that you've sewn by making a large cross-stitch with outside lines that emerge from the four inside holes (not the corner holes). On top of this cross, add another cross of the same size at the diagonals, forming a star-like configuration.

5. Attach the felt to the card with glue, and allow it to dry.

17

Felt Notepad Covers

Cover what is usually a mundane paper notepad with a felt sleeve. Glue on felt pieces or add a few simple embroidery stitches to create a unique gift to go on someone's desk or by their phone.

You Will Need for Each Pad

- Vertical paper notepad hinged with cardboard piece
- 2 pieces of felt in colors of your choice, each 9 x 12 inches (22.5 x 30 cm)
- Embroidery thread in colors of your choice
- Sewing thread to match felt
- Embroidery needle
- Pinking shears
- Straight pins
- Scissors
- Sewing machine
- Fabric glue, if decorating with felt pieces instead of embroidery

Instructions

1. Use pinking shears to cut out two rectangles of felt of the same color that are about 1 inch (2.5 cm) wider and longer than your notepad. (These pieces will be used for the back and flap.) Out of the other color of felt, cut out a piece of the same size with pinking shears, then cut 2 inches (5 cm) off the length with regular scissors. (This piece will be used to make a sleeve inside the back for holding the pad's cardboard backing.)

2. Overlap the back and flap pieces about ½ inch (1.3 cm) on one of the short edges (see figure on page 19).

DESIGNED BY
KAREN TIMM

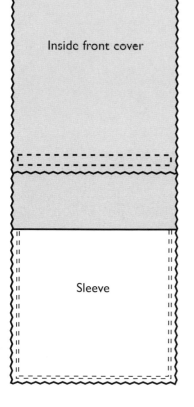

Inside front cover

Sleeve

Pin the two together with straight pins, and machine stitch them together with a rectangular-shaped line of stitches.

3. Sew the sleeve to the back around the edges with two lines of machine stitching about ¼ inch (6 mm) from the edge.

4. Decorate the front of your notepad with embroidery stitches or pieces of felt that you've cut into designs and glued on top.

Mosaic Frames

These lively frames are amazingly simple to make with a little patience and glue.

DESIGNED BY
PAT SAMUELS

You Will Need

- A variety of felt scraps in colors of your choice
- Pen or pencil
- Vanishing ink fabric marker
- Scissors
- Fabric glue or several sheets of double-sided adhesive that measure 5½ x 8¾ inches (13.8 x 21.9 cm)
- Flat-faced, 14½ x 16½ x 2-inch (36 x 41.3 x 5 cm) black frame, or other rectangular frame

Note: You can use glue or double-sided adhesive to attach felt pieces to your frame, or you can use a combination of both. Double-sided adhesive works well for attaching larger pieces; glue works well for attaching smaller pieces.

Instructions

1. Enlarge the patterns on page 116 to the size indicated, or a size that fits your frame.

2. Choose two or three colors that you'd like to use to make the main elements, or the fans, on the frame.

3. If using double-sided adhesive, pull off the slick side of about half a sheet and stick it to a scrap of felt of your choice. Repeat this process with the other colors you plan to use for the fans.

4. Use the pattern as a guide, and draw the pieces of the mosaic onto your pieces of felt with the vanishing marker in colors of your choice. Begin by drawing the center fan image.

5. Cut the pieces of the fan out of the felt, peel off the protective paper backing, and position them in place in the center of one of the long sides of the frame. (If using fabric glue instead of double-sided adhesive, draw the pieces onto the felt with the marker, cut them out, and glue them onto the frame.)

6. Add the two fans on either side using the same process. After positioning the fans, cut and add the triangular felt pieces that fit beneath and between the fans.

7. On top of the fans, cut and add small, repetitive accent pieces of felt. Next, cut out and attach the corner motifs.

8. Once you've positioned all of the fans and the corner pieces around the frame, cut out a variety of small felt squares in contrasting colors. Attach them in a random pattern between and around the main motifs.

Sunday Afternoon Sketch Book

Take this dressed-up sketch book to the museum, the park, or even the opera. It's functional as well as beautiful!

You Will Need

- Hardbound sketch pad with black cover (ours measures 9 × 12 inches [22.5 × 30 cm])
- 9 × 12-inch (22.5 × 30 cm) embossed gray felt, or size that fits the front of your notebook
- 9 × 12-inch (22.5 × 30 cm) embossed black felt
- Silver metallic embroidery thread
- Fabric glue
- Straight pins
- Small pair of scissors
- Sewing needle
- Chopstick or small paintbrush
- Package of variegated, colored beads

Instructions

1. Enlarge the patterns on page 115, and cut the shapes out of the embossed black felt.

2. Trim the gray felt to a size that fits the front of your notebook, leaving a narrow border of black around the edge.

3. Squeeze glue around the edges of the back of the gray piece of felt. Dot glue onto the other areas of the back of the piece. Gently smear the glue with a chopstick or the end of a small paintbrush.

DESIGNED BY
NICOLE TUGGLE

4. Flip the gray felt over, and position it on the front of your notebook. Press it in place.

5. Smear glue onto the back of each of the pieces of the design. Carefully place the pieces on the front, and press them in place.

6. After the felt pieces have dried, thread the needle with metallic thread. Sew each of the beads on one by one with small stitches into the felt. Tie off the thread when you reach the end of a line of beads

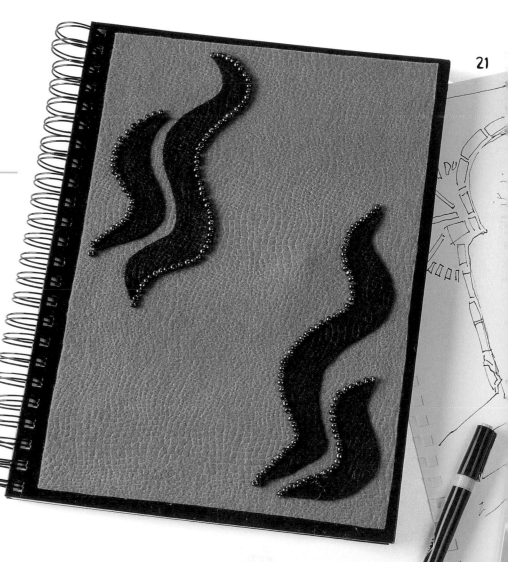

Marine Flag Wall Banner

The letters of the alphabet are spelled out in nautical flags on this bold banner. Makes a wonderful gift for any sea-lovin' soul!

DESIGNED BY
CAROLYNN WILLIAMS

You Will Need

▪ 36-inch (90 cm) width of the following: 2½ yards (2.25 m) white felt, 1 yard (90 cm) red felt, ¾ yard (67.5 cm) black felt

▪ 3 pieces of royal blue felt, each 9 × 12 inches (22.5 × 30 cm)

▪ 2 pieces of bright yellow felt, each 9 × 12 inches (22.5 × 30 cm)

▪ 2 yards (1.8 m) iron-on, medium-weight interfacing

▪ 5 yards (4.5 m) lightweight, iron-on fusible web

▪ 31½-inch-long (78.8 cm) piece of wooden lath with small hole drilled in center (for hanging)

▪ Vanishing ink fabric marker (optional)

▪ Heavyweight paper (optional)

▪ Scissors

▪ Rotary cutter and mat

▪ Straight pins

▪ Iron

Instructions

1. From the white felt, cut two pieces that measure 32½ × 37½ inches (81.3 × 93.8 cm) for the background of the banner, and two pieces that measure 6 × 15 inches (15 × 37.5 cm) for the banner's hanging sleeve.

2. Back one of the 32½ × 37½-inch (81.3 × 93.8 cm) white pieces with iron-on interfacing. Apply iron-on fusible web to the rest of the white felt and all of the other pieces of felt.

3. Cut 26 squares, each 4½ inches (11.3 cm), from the black felt. Cut two red felt strips that measure 32½ × 3 inches (81.3 × 7.5 cm) and 31½ × 3 inches (78.8 × 7.5 cm).

4. Enlarge the patterns for nautical symbols and alphabet flags on page 117 to the size indicated, and cut out pieces of felt in the designated colors. (To make this easier, trace the small pieces onto paper, cut them out, and then trace them with a vanishing ink fabric marker onto the felt. Use a rotary cutter and mat to cut the small pieces.)

5. After cutting out all of the pieces, arrange the black felt squares that you cut in step 3 on the right side of the interfaced white felt piece. Place them 4 inches (10 cm) from the edges, and ½ inch (1.3 cm) apart. When they're consistently placed, pin each in place. Iron each of the squares onto the background as you remove the pins.

6. Arrange the nautical symbols and alphabet flags on the black squares as you see them in the finished piece. After pinning them lightly, iron each in place, taking care to position each segment properly.

7. To form the framing border for the piece, iron on the red felt pieces: place the 32½-inch-long (81.3 cm) pieces on the top and bottom, then place the 31½-inch-long (78.8 cm) pieces between them on the two sides.

8. Flip the banner over, and apply 3-inch-wide (7.5 cm) strips of iron-on fusible web to the perimeter of the back of the front. Iron the remaining 32½ × 37½-inch (81.3 × 93.8 cm) white piece to the back.

9. To form the banner's hanging sleeve, iron a 2-inch-wide (5 cm) strip of fusible web along the long edge of each of the 6 × 15-inch (15 × 37.5 cm) white felt strips. Turn the pieces over and iron another 2-inch-wide (5 cm) strip of fusible web to the edge of the opposite side. With vanishing ink, mark a straight line 3 inches (7.5 cm) from the top edge of the back of the banner. Use this line to guide your placement of the bottom edge of one of the white strips. Leave a ½-inch (1.3 cm) margin between the strip and the banner's side edge, and iron the strip in place. Place the other white strip along the same line on the other side, leaving a ½-inch (1.3 cm) margin. After ironing the second strip in place, flip the sleeves over and up toward the top of the banner. Iron them in place to form a sleeve using the fusible web on the opposite side of the strips. Slip in the wooden lath, and hang the banner on a nail pushed through the small hole that you drilled in the lath.

Star Pillow

This handsome, unusual pillow will add a vivacious touch to a humdrum couch or chair.

24

DESIGNED BY
BARBARA MATTHIESEN

You Will Need

- ¼ yard (11.3 cm) of burgundy plush felt
- ¼ yard (11.3 cm) of blue-gray plush felt
- 8 x 24-inch (20 x 60 cm) piece of ivory plush felt
- 2½ yards (2.3 m) of ivory gimp trim (braided upholstery trim)
- 2 ivory or white buttons, each 1 inch (2.5 cm) in diameter
- Bag of polyester fiberfill
- Spool of ivory sewing thread
- Fabric glue
- Scissors
- Sewing pins and needle
- Sewing machine

Instructions

1. Enlarge the pattern on page 115 to the size indicated, and use it to cut out four pieces from the burgundy felt, four from the blue-gray felt, and two from the ivory felt.

2. Select two of the cut pieces in different colors, and place the right sides together. Pin the upper seams of the shapes together between the star symbol and the dot that you see on the pattern. Use a sewing machine threaded with ivory sewing thread to join the two pieces by sewing a ⅜-inch (9 mm) seam that runs from the star to the dot.

3. Add the other three diamond-shaped pieces in the same fashion to form a star, alternating the colors as you go.

4. After you've completed the first diamond, sew the second one, again alternating colors.

5. Pin the two star-shaped pieces together to form the front and back of the pillow with right sides facing each other.

6. Stitch a ⅜-inch (9 mm) seam around the star, leaving a 4-inch-wide (10 cm) opening on one star arm.

7. Trim the fabric close to the seam at the points of the star, and clip to the stitching line at the seams.

8. Turn the pillow right side out. Stuff it with fiberfill, making sure the points of the pillow are firmly stuffed. Slipstitch the opening closed.

9. Use fabric glue to attach gimp trim around the edge of the star at the seam.

10. Use embroidery floss or several strands of sewing thread to stitch a button to the center of the star on both sides. To do this, knot the end of your thread so that it doesn't pull through the button's hole, push your needle through a hole in one of the buttons, push the needle all the way through the pillow to the other side of it, then through a hole in the second button. Push your needle and thread back down through the hole on the other side of the button, return your needle through the pillow, and come back through the other hole. Continue this process until you've filled the holes. Pull the threads tightly, and repeat as needed to secure both buttons, and tuft the pillow.

Folk Art Banner

Debi Schmitz first designed this piece because she wanted a patriotic banner to hang on her door. You can also hang the banner out like a flag.

You Will Need

- 2⅓ yards (2.1 m) of denim-blue felt
- 1⅔ yards (1.5 m) of cranberry felt
- 2 yards (1.8 m) of antique white felt
- ¼ yard (22.5 cm) of butterscotch felt
- 5-yard (4.5 m) roll of light, iron-on adhesive (or fusible web)
- 28-inch-long (70 cm) wooden dowel, 1 inch (2.5 cm) wide
- #22 chenille needle, sharp
- 3 skeins, #5 black pearl cotton thread
- 7 assorted buttons
- 4 red buttons, 1 inch (2.5 cm) wide
- Straight pins
- Scissors
- Iron
- Pencil

Instructions

1. Cut out a piece of denim-blue felt and cranberry felt that each measure 24 x 54 inches (60 x 135 cm).

2. Cut out a 20 x 24-inch (50 x 60 cm) piece of denim-blue felt. Match the sides and top of this piece with those of the cranberry piece, and fuse them together with iron-on adhesive that covers all but a 1-inch (2.5 cm) border around the edge.

3. Enlarge the patterns on page 115 to the size indicated. Create serpentine stripes out of the antique white felt by repeating and joining outlines of pattern A in lengths. (The smallest stripes that fill the corners of the banner each measure approximately 11 inches [27.5 cm] long, the center stripe measures approximately 36 inches [90 cm] long, and the other two stripes measure approximately 26 inches [65 cm] long.) Cut each stripe a couple of inches longer than you need it, to allow for fitting it onto the banner.

4. Pin the longest stripe diagonally down the center of the banner, from the upper right corner to the lower left corner. Continue outward with the placement of the other four stripes, spacing them evenly. Iron them in place, and trim the edges to fit the sides of the banner. Use the chenille needle and black cotton thread to trim the sides of the stripes with a ½-inch (1.3 cm) blanket stitch (see page 114). Blanket-stitch along the bottom of the denim-blue square.

5. Iron the remaining adhesive to the back of the piece of butterscotch felt. Cut one large star from pattern B, and six small stars from pattern C. Position the stars on the banner as pictured in the finished piece, and iron them in place. With black thread, make long accent stitches that radiate from the stars onto the background. Sew a button in the center of each star.

6. Pin the striped banner face-up to the remaining piece of denim-blue felt. Blanket-stitch around the edges of the two pieces to create the finished banner.

7. Cut four 2 x 5-inch (5 x 12.5 cm) denim-blue strips of felt for the vertical straps. Fold one in half and overlap it on both sides of the banner about 2 inches (5 cm) in from the left side. Place the strip about 1½ inches (3.8 cm) down on the front and back of the piece. Evenly space and pin the other three strips in place along the top in the same position as the first. Stitch each in place by centering and sewing on a red button.

8. Slide the dowel into the banner straps.

Two Masterpieces in Felt

PAINTERLY WALL HANGING

This dramatic wall hanging is based upon a painting by Maurice de Vlaminck entitled *Tugboat at Chatou* (1906). Dana Irwin used small, cutout pieces of felt to represent brushstrokes in the final piece. Enlarge the drawing on page 29 below to create a piece similar to this one, or create a spin-off of your own favorite masterpiece!

DESIGNED BY
DANA IRWIN

You Will Need

- A color reproduction of a painting from a book, postcard, or poster
- Felt squares in colors that emulate the painting
- Large piece of felt for backing that is twice the size of your finished piece
- Tracing paper
- Pencil or pen
- Overhead projector (optional)
- Scissors
- Fabric marker or chalk
- Fabric glue
- Round dowel the width of your piece for hanging
- 2 screw eyes

Instructions

1. After choosing the image that you want to use, decide on the size of the wall piece that you plan to make, based on the proportions of the original photograph. (For instance, if you've chosen a rectangular image that measures 3 by 4 inches [7.5 × 10 cm], the final piece might measure 24 by 32 inches [60 × 80 cm].)

2. Enlarge the image with one of the following methods:

a. Cover the image with a piece of tracing paper, and trace the main lines of the image with a pencil or pen, as shown in Dana's drawing below. (Use this drawing if you want to make a wall hanging similar to ours.) Close in the lines so that they become shapes that can later be cut out of felt. Make color notations inside of the shapes for later reference. Use a copy machine to enlarge this drawing to the size that you want (you may need to piece together several enlarged sections).

b. Use an overhead projector to project the image onto a wall covered with a piece of paper that is at least as large as the final piece that you want to make. Outline the main lines of the image, and then create shapes with those lines. Make color notations within the shapes.

3. After the image is enlarged, trace a copy of it onto a large sheet of thin paper or several pieces of tracing paper that you've taped together. Number all of the shapes on the original image, and then repeat that on the copy so that you'll have a map of where your pieces should go.

4. Cut the shapes out of your original image one by one. Use the shapes as patterns to cut out pieces of felt in the appropriate colors. Use a fabric marker or chalk to number the back of each of the felt pieces with a number that corresponds to the one on the pattern.

5. Cut out a piece of neutral-colored felt (such as white, black, or tan) to be used as the backing for your piece. Cut it to twice the height of your piece and the same width.

6. Fold the piece in half so that the fold forms the top of your piece. Glue the wrong sides of the piece together with fabric glue, leaving a sleeve at the top large enough to insert your dowel for hanging.

7. Using the numbered map that you made earlier as a guide, lay out the pieces on the backing. After placing all of the pieces, glue them in place. Allow all parts to dry.

8. Insert a screw eye into each end of the dowel, and slide it into the sleeve at the top for hanging.

30

EMBELLISHED END TABLE

Use pieces of felt and braid to create a lavish, unconventional design on a tabletop. This design, created with the same process as the project on page 28, began with a decorative Japanese powder box that the designer bought on a trip. She enlarged the design, cut out the pieces, transferred them to the tabletop, and glued them in place.

To add more texture to the piece, she surrounded the design with borders of gold and colored braids. She used oil sticks to add highlights or color to certain areas of the design, such as the woman's hair and face.

DESIGNED BY
DANA IRWIN

Felt Quilt Earrings

These lightweight earrings made from scraps of felt are simple to make, and the possibilities for designs are infinite!

DESIGNED BY
ROSE SZABO

You Will Need for Each Pair

- Felt scraps in colors of your choice
- Beads small enough to fit on eye pins
- 1 pair of French wires (the wire that loops through the ear)
- 1 pair of eye pins (the wire to which you attach the beads)
- Fusible web
- Sequins (optional)
- Fabric glue or clear nylon thread
- Wire cutters
- Needle-nose pliers
- Scissors
- Iron

Instructions

1. Select several scraps of colored felt in colors of your choice for your earrings.

2. Iron fusible web onto the back of one of the scraps to use as the base for the earrings. Cut out four matching 1¼-inch (3.1 cm) felt squares. (Each earring has a front and back piece.)

3. Cut several squares of the same size from felt backed with fusible web to be used to create the "quilted" patterns of your earrings. For a simple way to make a design, cut the felt squares in half or on the diagonal, then in half again. When you do this, you'll create simple triangles and squares to use for making a pattern. You can overlap these pieces, or lay them out like a quilt. Add sequins for embellishment if you like.

4. Once you've positioned the pieces in the design of your choice, iron them in place on each of the four earring bases, keeping in mind that one side is the front of an earring and one side is the back.

5. Iron or glue the two base pieces of each earring together.

6. Sew or glue on beads or sequins for added sparkle.

7. To attach the beads and wires to the top of each earring, sew one looped end of an eye pin to the upper corner of each earring. Open the eye pin and slide on the beads. Cut away any extra wire length with the wire cutters. Then use the needle-nose pliers to close up each of the eye pins around the looped end of each of the French wires.

Fabulous Belt of Felt

Have absolutely nothing to wear? Transform a plain, white t-shirt with this belt that looks as if it took hours to make. In minutes you can clip, snip, and, finally, snap this belt into place. Favorable comments are guaranteed!

You Will Need

- Felt strip that is approximately 4 × 46 inches (10 × 115 cm)
- Scraps of embossed and plain felt in colors of your choice
- Scissors
- Cloth tape measure
- Fabric glue
- Small, round beads
- 2 strips of hook-and-loop tape, each about 2 inches (5 cm) wide
- Sewing needle and thread

Instructions

1. Take a measurement of your waist with the cloth tape measure. (Unfortunately, this is necessary.)

2. Add 2 inches (5 cm) to this measurement, and measure out a length of felt that corresponds to that number. Cut the strip of felt in a width that is slightly wider than the width that you want for your belt.

3. Trim the belt's edges with cuts that vary from wavy to jagged. Don't worry about the lines being perfect.

4. If you want to create abstract flowers for your belt, you can use a piece of embossed felt with a circular, spiraling pattern on it. Cut out several of the spirals, and use them as the center for your flowers. Cut out a couple of layers of petals to surround the center; layer the pieces, and then glue them in place with fabric glue. Sew on beads in the center.

5. Take other pieces of felt in colors that you like, and snip them into random pieces with your scissors. Don't plan the pieces, just snip away (close your eyes if you must!).

6. Make up playful designs with these pieces along the length of the belt. Overlap pieces, and move them until you come up with a design that you like. Glue them to the belt, and add more if you decide that you want more.

7. Trim the corners of one end of the belt at diagonals to create a point.

8. Position the belt around your waist, and overlap the pointed end. Use a straight pin to mark where the two ends overlap.

9. Sew the two pieces of hook-and-loop tape in place at this point to form a closure for the belt.

DESIGNED BY
BRENDA STAR

33

Bouncing Butterfly Pin

This elegant little pin will elicit compliments everywhere you go. It's not as complicated to make as it looks.

You Will Need

- Small squares of yellow and dark brown felt, each at least 5 inches (12.5 cm) square
- Yellow and orange embroidery thread, 1 skein each
- Newspaper
- Embroidery needle
- Small beads, buttons, or other embellishments of your choice
- Small piece of thin cardboard
- Three seed beads
- Several cosmetic cotton balls
- Scissors
- Fabric-dye-soaked rubber stamp pad, orange
- Small paintbrush
- Cosmetic tweezers (optional)
- Fabric glue
- 2-inch-long (5 cm) piece of covered wire
- 1½-inch-long (3.8 cm) pin back

DESIGNED BY
BARBARA EVANS

Instructions

1. Use the patterns on page 115 to cut out one set of wings from yellow felt, and the two parts of the butterfly's body from brown felt.

2. Thoroughly dampen the wings, and press them in a towel to remove the excess water. Place them on a surface covered with newspaper.

3. Dab some of the dye from the stamp pad around the edges of the wings using the small paintbrush. Allow it to dry, and apply another coat if needed. Set the wings aside to dry.

4. After the wings have dried, sew a decorative embroidery stitch, such as the blanket stitch (see page 114), around the edges with yellow or orange embroidery thread.

5. Use fabric glue to embellish the wings with beads, buttons, or small pieces of colored felt. Further embellish the wings with other embroidery stitches, if you choose.

Note: A basic buttonhole stitch (see page 114) can be used in several ways to make wing decorations. You can cut out small circles of felt, and stitch around the edges, adding beads to each stitch. You can also sew beads to the center of the felt circles. Because you are using heavy thread on tiny felt pieces, you may need to anchor the beginning and ending threads with fabric glue.

6. After embellishing the wings, use the pattern for the front of the body to cut out a small piece of cardboard of the same shape, but slightly smaller. Use fabric glue to attach the cardboard to it.

7. With the cardboard inside, place the two body pieces together to form the thorax of the butterfly. Sew the pieces together with orange thread using a blanket stitch or other decorative stitch. Begin at one side of the neck and work towards the tail. Sew one seed bead at the tip of the tail. (If the head of the needle you're sewing with is too thick to go through the bead, remove the needle from the thread, and push the thread through the bead without it. Then rethread the needle, and continue sewing.) When your stitching reaches the other side of the neck, use small bits of cotton to stuff the part of the body that is already sewn together. (Use a pair of tweezers to

push the cotton down inside the body, if needed.) Continue sewing around the head, adding a seed bead for an eye.

8. To form the antennae, bend the piece of wire into a U-shape, and place the bottom of the "U" between the two brown felt pieces at the top of the head. Add a small amount of cotton for stuffing. Sew between the two protruding pieces of wire to hold the antennae in place. Curl the ends of the wire into spirals, trimming any extra length off of the wire. Sew on another seed bead for the second eye.

9. Sew or glue a pin back onto the back of the body. Open up the pin, and glue the wings inside, on top of the pin bar. Press the wings down, allow them to dry, and then close up the pin.

Sassy Felt Shoes

Stop traffic with these gloriously gaudy shoes! These former bowling converted to party girl shoes are surprisingly simple to make. So grab your wildest felt scraps, and pink your way to a hip-hoppin' pair of footwear.

You Will Need

▌ One pair of cloth, lace-up shoes
▌ Scraps of felt in colors of your choice
▌ Tracing paper
▌ Pencil
▌ Pinking shears
▌ Fabric glue

Instructions

1. Press a piece of tracing paper against one side of your pair of shoes. Trace a rough outline of the flap and side of the shoe. Do the same for the tip of the shoe, and the other side. Although these patterns won't be perfect because of the curvature of the shoes, they will give you an idea of the size of felt pieces to cut.

2. Begin by covering the toe of the shoe. (We made our design symmetrical, but you can do a design out of any configuration of felt pieces.) To emulate our design, cut the triangular center piece out of felt first. Glue it on the shoe, and then cut the strips that fit on either side of it. Trim and adjust pieces to fit as you go along.

3. Following the contours of the shoe that you've determined with your rough patterns, cut the side pieces to fit. (If you want your design to be the same on the other side, cut two pieces that are identical.)

4. Add the pieces that go on the back tab and the tongue of the shoe.

5. Cut and glue on the accent pieces that go on the tip and flaps last.

DESIGNED BY
ELLEN ZAHOREC

Scrap String Purses

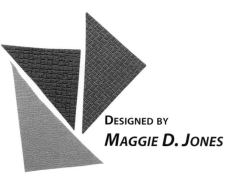

These purses are so lovely, nobody will dream that you made them from leftover felt scraps!

DESIGNED BY
MAGGIE D. JONES

You Will Need

- Scraps of felt in colors of your choice (we used several embossed felts)
- Length of cord that measures approximately 40-45 inches (100-112.5 cm) long for strap
- Decorative buttons
- 3 inches (7.5 cm) of hook-and-loop tape for purse closure
- Several sheets of blank paper
- Ruler or other straightedge
- Pencil
- Vanishing ink fabric marker
- Scissors
- Sewing machine
- Masking tape

Instructions

1. On a blank piece of paper, draw a rectangle that measures 7½ × 4 inches (18.8 × 10 cm) and one that measures 5 × 4 inches (12.5 × 10 cm). Cut out the rectangles, which will be used as the patterns for sizing the pieces of your scrap purse.

2. Take the smaller rectangle, and position it on top of the larger one, matching the bottom edges. Fold over the top of the piece of the larger rectangle to form a flap.

3. Use the ruler and a pencil to draw diagonal or other lines of your choice on both the front and back of the paper patterns, forming a quilt-like design. Cut out the pieces of your pattern along the lines that you've drawn.

4. Use the vanishing ink marker to trace these pattern pieces onto scraps of felt in colors of your choice. Cut out the pieces, allowing an extra ¼ inch (6 mm) beyond any traced lines that form overlapping seams on the purse. (You don't need to make this allowance along the lines that form the outside edges of the purse).

5. Position the pieces of your purse on a surface to form the 7½ x 4-inch (18.8 x 10 cm) rectangle and the 5 x 5-inch (12.5 x 10 cm) rectangle with which you began, overlapping the edges where the various pieces join. Sew the pieces together along these overlapping seams with zigzag stitching in various colors.

6. Reposition the two rectangles as they were in step 2, and fold them together to form a back, front, and a flap for your purse. With the flap positioned up, sew up the sides, bottom, and along the edges of the flap with a zigzag stitch.

7. Cut off a 1-inch-long (2.5 cm) piece of hook-and-loop tape, and hand stitch one half of it in position along the top edge of the front of the bag, and the other half underneath the flap, so that the two will form a closure for the bag.

8. Secure the ends of one of the pieces of cord by wrapping a narrow piece of masking tape around each so that they won't ravel. Hand stitch the two ends of the cord on the underside of the flap right above the top edge of the purse's front, so that the ends are hidden when you close the purse.

9. Close the purse, and sew on a decorative button or two of your choice.

Variation of flap: For an alternative to the squared-off flap, cut the flap ½ inch (1.3 cm) longer, allowing room to trim off the edges of the flap at diagonals to make a pointed flap. Sew a button onto the tip of the flap.

Rose-Clad Felt Hat

Take a plain felt hat and make it into an accessory that any Annie Hall would be proud to wear.

You Will Need

- Floppy hat sewing pattern of your choice with notions, or readymade felt hat
- 9 x 12-inch (22.5 x 30 cm) felt pieces in the following colors: 2 dark red, 2 hot pink, 2 dark green
- Wax candle and matches
- Scissors
- Tongs or long-handled tweezers
- Needle and heavy thread
- Sewing machine (if making your own hat)

Instructions

1. If you want to sew your own hat, buy beige felt in the amount indicated on the pattern that you choose. Cut and sew the hat according to the directions.

2. To make the dark red flowers, cut the dark red felt into five 3½-inch (1.3 cm) squares and three 3-inch (7.5 cm) squares. Diagonally trim off the corners on the squares.

38

3. Light the wax candle. Use the tongs to hold the edge of one of the felt squares about an inch (2.5 cm) above the candle flame. As the edge of the felt begins to melt, continue to turn the felt as the edges begin to turn under. (Do not hold the felt in the flame because the edge will turn black.)

4. Continue this process, and singe all of the dark red pieces of felt.

5. Fold one of the singed 3½-inch (8.8 cm) petals in half, then roll it up tightly so that it forms the center of the flower. Hand stitch the bottom of it with several long stitches to hold the roll in place.

6. To form the next surrounding row of petals, attach the dark red 3-inch (7.5 cm) petals. Turn the curled edges to the outside, and attach the three petals to the center of the flower around the base with long stitches.

7. Add the remaining four 3½-inch (8.8 cm) petals in the same manner, and sew them in place.

8. Use the same steps to make a slightly smaller rose with five 3-inch (7.5 cm) squares and three 2½-inch (6.3 cm) squares cut from the hot pink felt.

9. Cut several 3½-inch (8.8 cm) squares out of green felt. Trim them into wide leaf shapes, and singe the edges. Sew them to the base of the flowers.

10. Fold back the brim of the hat, making an area wide enough for placing the flowers. Sew the flowers and leaves to the brim of your hat with long stitches through both the brim and the hat.

39

DESIGNED BY
VIVIAN PERRITTS

Snakeskin Bag

This sexy, dress-up bag makes the most of today's embossed felts.
And no snakes were harmed in the processs of making it!

You Will Need

- 3 pieces of black, "snakeskin," embossed felt, each
  9 x 12 inches (22.5 x 30 cm)
- 2 pieces of brown, floral-patterned, embossed felt,
  each 9 x 12 inches (22.5 x 30 cm)
- Skein of #5 black pearl cotton thread
- 3 black buttons, ⅝ inches (1.6 cm) wide
- Black sewing thread
- 1½ yards (1.4 m) black cord, ½ inch
  (1.3 cm) wide
- Sewing needle
- Chenille needle
- Scissors

40

DESIGNED BY
NANCY WORRELL

Instructions

1. Using the photograph of the finished bag as a guide, follow the lines of the embossed pattern on one of the brown felt pieces to cut an uneven, scalloped edge at a diagonal. (Begin about 1½ inches [3.8 cm] from the top, and cut a diagonal that ends at around 5½ inches [13.8 cm] down.) Save the piece of felt that you've cut away.

2. From the saved piece, trim away a piece about 1½ inches (3.8 cm) wide along the same diagonal as the larger piece. The piece that remains will form the brown piece that goes in the corner.

3. From the other 9 x 12-inch (22.5 x 30 cm) brown felt piece, cut out three embossed flowers.

4. Place the larger piece of cut brown felt right side up on top of one of the black, snakeskin felt pieces. Align the edges, and pin or baste in place.

5. Thread the chenille needle with the black cotton thread. Use a blanket stitch (see page 114) to attach the brown piece to the black piece along the curved inside edge only. Remove any stitches or pins.

6. Position the smaller brown piece of felt in the corner of the same piece, align the edges, and pin or baste it in place. Blanket-stitch it in place along the curved edge as you did the larger piece. Remove any stitches or pins.

7. Flip the black piece with attached brown pieces over, so that the wrong side is face up. Position another black felt piece, embossed side up, on top of it (wrong sides together). Align the bottom edges.

8. Fold the third piece of black felt in half, wrong sides together, to form a 9 x 6-inch (22.5 x 15 cm) rectangle. Form a pocket for the purse by aligning this piece with the bottom and side edges of the black felt piece that you placed in step 7. Baste or pin both black pieces in place.

9. Blanket-stitch around the edges of the bag so that the brown felt pieces and the three black felt pieces are sandwiched together. After sewing, remove pins or basting threads.

10. Place the three flowers on the front of the bag. Use the sewing needle and black thread to tack the flowers in place with three black buttons.

11. Cut the black cord to the length that you'd like it for the strap of your purse. Cut it, and knot the ends. Tuck the ends of the cord inside the pocket edges. Sew them in place with a needle and black thread.

Soft 'n Classy Hats

Plush felts are perfect to combine with textured fabrics in a hat. The crowns of these hats are pieced and appliquéd. Each hat is designed to fit a medium-sized woman's head.

42

DESIGNED BY
MARGARET GREGG

You Will Need

- Swatches of felt and fabric of your choice
- ⅓ yard (11.9 cm) of lining fabric
- 25-inch-wide (62.5 cm) grosgrain ribbon for inner band
- Sewing thread
- Rotary cutter with straight blade and mat (optional)
- Straight pins
- Fabric glue
- Scissors
- Sewing machine

Instructions

1. Choose your palette of felt and fabrics. We included some velvet, tapestry, and metallics. Experiment with various stitches and piece together small swatches of the fabrics to understand how they will perform in relationship to one another.

2. Enlarge the patterns on page 116 to the size indicated. Choose a crown design (see suggestions below), and cut out pieces of fabric to resemble it, allowing a ⅜-inch (9 mm) seam for all overlapping edges. Overlay the pieces, and pin them in place. Top stitch them together with your sewing machine. Trim the edges into a circle that matches the crown pattern.

3. Use the crown and stand patterns to cut pieces out of the lining fabric with a ⅜-inch (9 mm) seam allowance.

4. Cut the hat stand out of a coordinating fabric. Top stitch the stand with free-form, curved lines to create a quilted effect.

5. Pin either end of the outer stand together with right sides facing, and sew the seam together. Clip the top edge of the stand with ½-inch (1.3 cm) vertical slits spaced about ½ inch (1.3 cm) apart. Pin the stand to the crown's outer edge with right sides together. Sew together with a ⅜-inch (9 mm) seam.

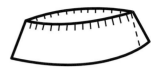

6. Turn the piece right-side-out, and top stitch along the crown/stand seam line.

7. Assemble the crown/stand lining using the same process as described in step 5. With wrong sides together, straight stitch the lining to the bottom inside edge of the hat.

8. Use the brim pattern with a ⅜-inch (9 mm) seam allowance added for the top of the brim and the bottom. Pin the two pieces together with the right sides facing and the seams matching. Sew the outer edges with a ⅜-inch (9 mm) seam, and turn the brim right side out. Top stitch around the outer edge. Add a couple of concentric rows of circular stitching inside this edge for both decorative and structural purposes. Clip the inside edge of the brim all the way around with ½-inch (1.3 cm) slits.

9. Pin the stand to the brim with right sides facing, adjusting it to fit. Sew it into place. Stitch the outer edge of the piece of ribbon into place along the seam line at the bottom of the crown.

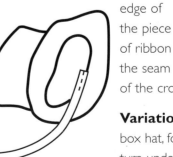

Variation: To make a pillbox hat, follow steps 1-6, and turn under the edges of the lining before top stitching it.

43

Reverse Appliqué Vest

This colorful vest uses a clever appliqué process to create a romantic, medieval look.

DESIGNED BY
KAREN M. BENNETT

You Will Need

- Bolero vest sewing pattern with yardages of purple and hot pink felt for making front and back
- Skein of hand-dyed, variegated purple pearl cotton thread, size 12 (see suppliers' list on page 128)
- 2 skeins of hand-dyed French cotton thread (see suppliers' list on page 128)
- Straight pins
- Wavy rotary blade, cutter, and mat
- Freezer paper
- Clothes iron
- Sewing machine
- Thread
- Size 15 sewing machine needles
- Extra bobbin case for sewing machine
- Empty thread spool
- Appliqué scissors

Instructions

1. Cut out two sets of the pieces of the vest pattern, one in purple felt and one in hot pink felt. Sew the shoulder seams of the purple pieces together. Repeat for the pink version.

2. Place the two pieces together on a large table with the wrong sides together. Pin the armhole seams and the edges of the vest together.

3. Enlarge the braided rosette pattern on page 116 to the size indicated, and make two extra copies of it. Trace the design onto the dull side of the freezer paper. Set the iron on a low temperature, and iron the paper onto the center of the back of the purple vest (the shiny side of the paper will stick with heat).

4. Wind a portion of the hand-dyed pearl cotton thread onto an empty spool, and thread the top of your sewing machine with it. Thread the sewing machine bobbin with French cotton thread.
Note: When using a thicker thread in the bobbin, you will need to adjust the bobbin's tension. To do this, turn the large screw in your bobbin to the left to loosen the tension. The tension should be adjusted to the point that when the bobbin is dangled by the thread and shaken slightly, it falls for a couple of inches and stops.

5. To begin sewing the rosette, lengthen your stitch length to 4 on your sewing machine. (Don't change the tension setting.) Take one stitch and bring the bobbin's thread to the top. Choose a point on the rosette's chain and begin stitching around the design. (If you have a needle stop-down option on your machine, engage it. This will prevent your work from sliding around as you sew and maneuver the curves.) Repeat for the other chains, remembering to bring the lower thread to the top first.

8. To sew the flower in the center, begin by sewing the circle in the middle. Work your way out to the petals, always bringing the lower bobbin thread to the top.

9. Trace two outlines of the center flower design from the pattern onto the freezer paper. Cut them out of the paper, and iron the small flower patterns onto each front section of the vest. Repeat the sewing process for these patterns that you used on the rosette.

10. When the sewing is complete, remove the freezer paper. Use appliqué scissors to carefully cut the sections of purple felt away, clipping almost to the edge of the sewing. Be cautious not to cut any of the threads.

11. Knot the threads brought up to the top. Using a large needle, hide the threads inside the two layers of felt.

12. Cut about ⅜ inch (9 mm) off of the armholes with the rotary cutter fitted with a wavy blade.

13. Sew the purple side seams only, right sides together. Trim the seam.

14. On the pink side, fold the raw edges under and hand whip them together with regular sewing thread.

15. Select a serpentine stitch on your machine. Rethread the machine with hand-dyed threads for both upper and lower threads.

16. Machine stitch about ½ inch (1.3 cm) in from the edge of the armholes. Stitch the outer edge of the vest using a 1-inch (2.5 cm) seam allowance, then trim about ⅜ inch (9 mm) off of the edges of the vest with the rotary cutter and wavy blade.

Colorful Stitched String Purse

Variegated purple threads blend with light and dark purple cord to make a stunning surface treatment for this felt purse. Wow!

You Will Need

- 8 x 10-inch (20 x 25 cm) piece of purple felt
- 2 skeins of hand-dyed, variegated purple pearl cotton thread, size 5 (see page 128 for supplier)
- 4 yards (3.6 m) of dark purple silk cord
- 2 yards (1.8 m) of light purple silk cord
- 6-inch-long (15 cm) piece of beaded fringe
- Button for closure
- Spool of 40 weight rayon sewing thread
- Smoke-colored nylon sewing thread
- Wavy rotary cutter blade
- Rotary cutter and mat
- Chalk marker
- Sewing machine with couching foot
- Sewing needle and thread
- Fabric glue
- Straight pins

DESIGNED BY
KAREN M. BENNETT

Instructions

1. Enlarge the patterns on page 116 to the size indicated. Use the wavy rotary blade to cut them out of purple felt.

2. Place the two pieces together, and drop the flap over the top to understand how the purse will look after it is sewn. Keeping this placement in mind, use the chalk marker to freehand draw three sets of overlapping lines that run from the bottom of the back of the purse over the flap, leaving a ¼-inch (6 mm) margin at the edges for placing a seam later. Draw three sets of lines that correspond roughly with the first set of lines on the front of the purse.

3. Wind the skeins of hand-dyed thread onto two spools so that the threads will be allowed to move freely as you sew. Thread the sewing machine and bobbin with the smoke-colored nylon thread. Place the couching foot on your machine. (If you don't have one, use the universal foot. You will have to guide the thread yourself, rather than letting the foot feed the thread for you.)

4. Feed each strand of the thread through the hole in the top of the couching foot. Set the machine for a ⅛-inch-wide (3 mm) zigzag stitch. Couch over the variegated threads with the nylon thread. (Follow the chalk-marked lines, not the thread.) When sewing the middle set of loops that move from the back over to the front of the flap, form a loop of thread at the end of the first line that can serve as the button loop. Continue back in the other direction with the completion of the line.

5. When you've completed the couching, thread a large needle with the ends of the pearl cotton. Pull the threads to the back of the fabric, and tie them off in knots. Repeat this process with the nylon thread.

6. Cut the dark purple silk cord in half. Braid together two 2-yard (1.8 m) lengths of dark purple silk cord and the 2-yard (1.8 m) length of light purple silk cord. Sew over the ends to secure the cords together, and make a strap for the purse.

7. Use fabric glue to attach the length of beaded fringe to the lower inside edge of the purse's back piece.

8. Pin the front piece to the back piece with the ends of the strap enclosed in the corners of the purse's upper edge. Sew a ¼-inch (6 mm) seam around the edge with rayon thread, using a triple straight stitch for strength.

9. Sew on the button with pearl cotton, and place the purse's loop around it.

Splashy Martini Skirt

Our version of the "mature" woman's poodle skirt will make you the supreme hostess at your next party. Shake and pour, baby!

DESIGNED BY
CAROLYNN WILLIAMS

You Will Need

FOR THE SKIRT:

■ Wide, circular skirt pattern of your choice with notions

■ Yardage of pink wool felt to accommodate skirt pattern

FOR THE APPLIQUÉ:

■ 8 x 12-inch (30 x 20 cm) piece of gray felt

■ 4 x 7-inch (10 x 17.5 cm) piece of white felt

■ Scraps of olive green and red felt

■ ½ yard (45 cm) lightweight, iron-on adhesive

■ ⅛ yard (11.3 cm) iron-on vinyl

■ One package of medium-sized bugle beads, silver metallic

■ Transparent nylon thread

■ Silver metallic thread

■ Pen

■ Beading needle

■ Hand sewing needle

■ Scissors

■ Iron

■ Sewing machine

Instructions

1. Cut out the pieces of the skirt using the pattern that you've chosen.

2. Cover the backs of the gray and white felt pieces with iron-on adhesive. Do not remove the paper from the adhesive.

3. Enlarge the patterns on page 116 to the size indicated. Trace the shaker pattern in reverse on the back of the prepared gray felt with the pen. Cut out the shaker. Repeat this process to cut out the cocktail glass.

4. Lay the front of the unsewn skirt out on a large surface. Position the appliqués near the bottom of the skirt. Position the beaker so that it appears to be pouring into the glass. Remove the paper from the back

of each of the appliqués, and iron them into place on the skirt.

5. Use the patterns to cut the olive out of green felt and the pimento out of red felt. Position them on the glass.

6. Using the pattern for the glass, cut the shape out of the iron-on vinyl. Remove the paper backing, then lay the sticky side of the vinyl over the glass and olive. Place the removed paper backing on top of the vinyl to protect it, then iron it in place.

7. Satin stitch with silver metallic thread by hand or machine around the edge of the glass and shaker.

8. Thread the beading needle with the transparent nylon thread, and sew on the bugle beads one by one that curve from the glass to the beaker. To do this, pull the thread up from the back of the skirt, thread a bead onto the needle and thread, pull it down to the front of the skirt, and then push the thread through to the back side. Repeat this process, using one continuous thread pulled from the back to the front at points where you want the beads to appear. (You do not need to use an embroidery hoop. The felt has enough body that it is not necessary. Just be sure not to pull the thread too tightly between beads or the area could pucker.)

9. Complete the construction of the skirt following your pattern instructions.

Male and Female Cockatiels

Perch a couple of these felt birds on a shelf, in a bird cage, or even on top of your computer. They'll put a smile on your face every time you look at them!

You Will Need for One Pair of Birds

▌ 9 x 12-inch (22.5 x 30 cm) piece of bright yellow felt

▌ Approximately 2 square feet (60 cm) of off-white plush felt and gray plush felt

▌ 9 x 12-inch (22.5 x 30 cm) piece of white felt

▌ Small scraps of black, orange, and gray felt for features

▌ 2 gray pipe cleaners, each 12 inches (30 cm) long

▌ Fusible web

▌ Iron

▌ Sewing machine

▌ Small bag of cotton balls or polyester fiberfill

▌ Fabric glue (optional)

Instructions

1. Enlarge the patterns on page 120 to the size indicated. Fold the gray plush felt in half, wrong sides together, and cut out four of the body by following the outline of the pattern, and two tails. Cut the tails down the middle to form four long pieces. Fold the yellow felt, and cut

DESIGNED BY
ROSE SZABO

out two of the head pattern (separate the outline of the head from the body) for the male bird. From the off-white plush felt, cut out four wings, and two tails.

2. Iron fusible web onto the 9 x 12-inch (22.5 x 30 cm) piece of white felt and the scraps of orange, black, and gray felt. From the white felt cut out four wing borders, from the orange cut out four cheeks and four beaks, and from the black cut out four eyes. Iron the eyes and the cheeks onto the sides of the two yellow head pieces, and in the same positions on the sides of the two gray body pieces. Iron the white border pieces onto the four wings.

3. To make the male cockatiel, iron the yellow head onto the gray body with fusible web, or use fabric glue to attach it.

4. Stitch the wings onto both bodies using the wing placement guides on the pattern.

5. Use a sewing machine to stitch the halves of the birds together with the wrong sides together, beginning and ending at the dots on the pattern.

6. Bunch the three tail pieces for each bird together with the two gray pieces on the bottom and the off-white piece on the top. Stitch together the ends of these pieces at the top. Insert the sewn end of each tail at the top of the opening that has been left unstitched on the body. Hand or machine sew the tails in place.

7. Iron on the parts of the beak that go on either side of heads, taking care to line them up evenly.

8. Stuff the birds gently with cotton or fiberfill. Hand or machine sew up the openings where you stuffed the birds.

9. Cut small slits in the body for inserting the feet. To make the feet, cut a 12-inch (30 cm) gray pipe cleaner in half, then fold each of the halves to form 3-inch-long (7.5 cm) doubled pieces for the legs. Cut another pipe

cleaner in quarters to form 3-inch (7.5 cm) pieces for the feet. Turn under the ends of the feet about ⅛ inch (3 mm), so that they won't be sharp. Twist the ends of the longer pieces, or legs, around the feet, then twist the leg pieces together. Insert the bend at the top of each leg inside the body of the bird. If necessary, apply glue at the intersection of the leg and bird.

11. To make the accessories, do the following:

a. For the scarf, extend the pattern to cut a 12-inch-long (30 cm) scarf. Fringe the ends, then tie it around the neck of the bird.

b. To make the top hat, cut out a piece of black felt for the side of the hat measuring 2 x 5 inches (5 x 12.5 cm). Use the patterns to cut out the brim and the top from black felt. Sew the top by hand to one of the long edges of the side. (Pull the edge of the side around the circumference of the circle that forms the top as you stitch.) Stitch the side edges together where they join. Sew the flat brim to the other edge of the sides to form the hat. Place it on the head of one of the birds.

Moon and Stars Window Valance

T his imaginative valance makes a sweet adornment for a child's room. Our version is made for a 4-foot-long (1.2 m) curtain rod, but you can vary the size according to your needs.

DESIGNED BY
KIM TIBBALS-THOMPSON

You Will Need

▌ 1 yard (90 cm) blue felt, 54 inches (135 cm) wide
▌ ½ yard (45 cm) yellow felt, 36 inches (90 cm) wide
▌ ¼ yard (22.5 cm) white felt, 36 inches (90 cm) wide
▌ Skein of yellow yarn
▌ 2 yards (1.8 m) yellow braid trim
▌ 2 yards (1.8 m) white fringe trim
▌ Fusible web hem tape
▌ 6 to 9 cotton balls
▌ Measuring tape
▌ Fabric scissors

▌ Pinking shears
▌ Vanishing ink fabric marker
▌ Blue sewing thread
▌ Large sewing needle for yarn
▌ Fabric marker
▌ Glue gun
▌ Sewing machine

Instructions

1. Cut a rectangle of blue felt that measures 24 x 50 inches (60 x 125 cm). Press under 1 inch (2.5 cm) along both short sides and one long side, and fuse into place with the hem tape.

2. Fold the rectangle in half to form a 23 x 24-inch (57.5 x 60 cm) square. Use the measuring tape to mark the spot along the fold that is 12 inches (30 cm) from the fused edge of the piece. Draw a graceful curve by hand from that point to the lower opposite corner. Use scissors to cut through both fabric thicknesses along this line which forms the arc of your valance.

3. Use pinking shears to cut out nine blue felt tabs that measure 3 x 7 inches (7.5 x 17.5 cm). Fold each tab in half to make 3 x 3½-inch (7.5 x 8.8 cm) squares. Evenly pin the ends of the tabs 1 inch (2.5 cm) down from the top edge of the valance on the back side. To hold the tabs in place, use blue sewing thread to machine stitch a ½-inch (1.3 cm) seam through the tabs along the top edge.

4. Hot glue the white fringe trim along the bottom edge of the valance, then glue the yellow trim on top. Wrap the raw edges of the trims around the back of the valance, and glue in place.

5. Enlarge the patterns on page 118 to the size indicated. Cut two moons out of yellow felt with pinking shears. On the front of the moon, use the pattern as a guide for marking the eyebrow, nostril, eye, and mouth with the vanishing ink marker. Backstitch by hand along these lines with a single strand of yellow yarn. Place the front and back of the moon together, and hand sew the edges with the blanket stitch (see page 114) at ½-inch (1.3 cm) intervals around the moon.

6. Cut the stars out of white felt with pinking shears: three small, eight medium, and one large. (You'll use a single thickness of felt for the stars on the valance, and a double thickness for any stars that are suspended.)

7. Refer to the finished piece as a guide, and position the moon and stars on the valance. Attach the moon to the valance by tacking it with glue in several places. Lightly tack the stars in place with hot glue. Using a single strand of yellow yarn and ½-inch-long (1.3 cm) dash-like stitches, attach the stars to the valance at the points and corners.

8. To make the three suspended stars, use a single strand of yellow yarn, and stitch two thicknesses of stars at all of the points and corners but two with a ½-inch (1.3 cm) stitch. Tie each stitch off at the back, and clip it. Stuff each star with a couple of cotton balls before adding two last stitches that close the form. Seal the final point with a stitch made with a length of yarn that is tied at the top of the point and then attached to the back of the valance with hot glue to create a swinging star.

Hoedown Angels

These down-to-earth angels make a great gift for anyone with a child's heart.

DESIGNED BY
BETTY AUTH

You Will Need for Both Dolls

▌ 1 yard (90 cm) flesh-colored felt

▌ ½ yard (45 cm) off-white embossed felt

▌ 9 x 12-inch (22.5 x 30 cm) piece of denim blue embossed felt

▌ 9 x 12-inch (22.5 x 30 cm) piece of pale yellow embossed felt

▌ 9 x 12-inch (22.5 x 30 cm) piece of burgundy embossed felt

▌ 5 x 5-inch-square (12.5 x 12.5 cm) piece of embossed felt

▌ 3 silk ribbon flowers, each 1 inch (2.5 cm) wide

▌ 4 round black beads, each ¼ inch (6 mm)

▌ 2 white shirt buttons

▌ Polyester fiberfill

▌ Fabric scissors

▌ Pinking shears

▌ Sewing needle

▌ Straight pins

▌ Pink chalk or "blush" (facial makeup)

▌ Soft paintbrush or makeup brush (optional)

▌ Off-white and black sewing thread

▌ Purple vanishing ink marker

▌ Sewing machine

Instructions

1. Enlarge the patterns on page 119 to the size indicated, and cut out the shapes. Place the patterns for the doll bodies on the right sides of the piece of folded, flesh-colored felt. Trace around the patterns with the vanishing marker, and cut two of each pattern.

2. Machine sew the two layers together with a narrow seam. Use the fabric scissors to trim the felt close to the seam all the way around each of the shapes. Cut a small slit in the back of each doll through one layer of felt, and stuff the dolls lightly with the polyester fiberfill. Hand stitch the slits closed. (You'll cover this slit later with clothing pieces.)

3. Trace the wings onto the embossed side of the folded, off-white felt with the vanishing marker. Sew a narrow seam around the edges. Trim the seam to about ¼ inch (6 mm) with pinking shears.

4. Referring to the pattern, machine stitch lines across the top of the arms and legs as indicated by dashed lines on the patterns.

5. Thread the sewing needle with about 24 inches (60 cm) of doubled black thread. Make a big knot in the end of the thread. Calculate where the eye should go on the face of each body, and poke the needle through the face from the back side. Leave the knot in the thread hanging about an inch (2.5 cm) on the back.

6. Pick up a round black bead, and slide it down the thread. Poke the needle back through the front side of the face, close to the hole. Slide the bead down to the felt as you pull the thread to the back side, leaving some slack in the thread. Pull the needle back through to the front of the face, close to the bead. Push it through the bead again, then to the back. Pick up another bead with your needle at that point.

7. With the needle in one hand, use the other hand to grasp the hanging knot. Pull both beads up tightly, causing an indentation in the face of the doll and securing the beads to the face. Snuggle the eyes in by pulling the threads tightly, then tie a knot in the thread close to the bead. (Cut the needle off of the thread if it makes this easier.) Clip the ends of the threads.

8. To delineate the cheeks, use a soft makeup brush, paintbrush, or wad of cotton to dust pink chalk or makeup blush on the cheeks of the dolls.

9. Cut the girl's skirt from pale yellow felt. Hand or machine sew a gathering line with long straight stitches, about ¼ inch (6 mm) apart, along one of the long sides of the strip. Position the strip around the doll's waist with the ends at her back. Pull the threads and gather the skirt to fit the waist of the doll. Secure the skirt with a couple of stitches, then sew it to the doll's waist.

10. To make the vest, use the pattern to cut one vest from the burgundy felt. Use pinking shears to trim the curved edge of the vest. With right sides facing, sew the vest together at the sides with a narrow seam. After sewing, turn the vest right side out. Put the vest on the doll, and tack the edges together with needle and thread at the center front.

11. Use the pattern to cut the girl's hair from pale yellow felt. Use the scissors to make repeated 1¾-inch (4.4 cm) cuts, about ¼ inch (6 mm) apart along one long edge of the strip. Use long stitches to hand gather along the uncut edge, and pull up the threads until the hair fits on the head in a full, floppy fringe. Sew the hair to the top of the doll's head.

12. Sew or glue two silk flowers to the head, covering the bottom of the fringe. Attach another flower in the center of the front of the vest. Sew or glue the angel wings to the doll's back, hiding the opening where she was stuffed.

13. From denim blue felt, cut out one front, one back, two straps, and two pockets for the boy doll. Trim the bottoms of the pant legs on both the front and back pieces with pinking shears. Pink the top edges of both pockets and the ends of the straps. Use the sewing machine to topstitch with off-white thread across the tops of the pockets, around the edge of the bib, and along the outside edges of the straps.

14. Position the front and back pieces of the overalls together, and machine sew the side edges with a ¼-inch (6 mm) seam of off-white thread. Place the pointed end of the straps inside the top back edge (waist) of the pants and tack the edge to the pants with needle and thread. Pull the pants onto the doll. Tack them in place on the doll with a couple of small stitches. Fold the straps over to the front, and attach them to the overalls on the front by sewing on two white shirt buttons.

15. Cut the cap circle and bill out of embossed brown felt. Stitch a gathering line around the circle, and pull it up so that it fits on the head. Secure and tie off the thread. Slip the bill under one edge of the cap, and glue or sew it in place. Place the cap on the doll's head, and sew it in place by hand with a few small stitches.

16. Cut a 2-inch-square (5 cm) piece of pale yellow felt, and fringe it as you did the girl doll's hair. Roll up the fringe, and sew or glue it under the bill of the cap. Trim the ends.

17. Sew or glue the doll's wings to the back of the overalls.

ABRACADABRA
Rabbit in a Hat

This clever puppet that pops in and out of a hat is made from a yogurt carton, felt, cardboard, and some beads.

DESIGNED BY
MONA-KATRI MAKELA

You Will Need

- 9 x 12-inch (22.5 x 30 cm) sheet of red, adhesive-backed felt
- 3 sheets of black, adhesive-backed felt, each 9 x 12 inches (22.5 x 30 cm)
- ½ yard (45 cm) plain, white felt
- Scrap of red felt
- 9 x 12-inch (22.5 x 30 cm) sheet of plain yellow felt
- 32 ounce (960 mL) plastic yogurt container
- Sheet of thin cardboard, at least 8 inches (20 x 20 cm) square
- 16 inches (40 cm) black elastic cord
- Black sewing thread
- White sewing thread
- Handful of polyester fiberfill or cotton
- 3 small purple beads (nose)
- 2 small black beads (eyes)
- ¼-inch (6 mm) red button
- Lettering stencil with alphabet letters that measure 1 to 1½ inches (2.5-3.75 cm) high
- Sewing needle
- Scissors
- Craft knife
- Black pen
- Drawing compass
- Fabric glue

Instructions

1. Enlarge the patterns on page 118 to the size indicated. Cut out the rabbit's ears, head, arms, and body from white felt. Set them aside.

2. Cut the bottom off the yogurt container with the craft knife. Remove the paper backing from one of the sheets of black, adhesive-backed felt, and place it adhesive side up on your work surface. Position the container lengthwise along the 9-inch (22.5 cm) edge, and slowly roll it over the felt. Trim the felt with the scissors where the edges meet, and press it in place. Then trim the excess felt away from the top and bottom edges, leaving about an ⅛ inch (3 mm) extra on both ends. Fold this allowance inside the container on both ends.

3. Fold the piece of felt for the rabbit's body in half along the dotted line on the pattern. Cut a 1½-inch (3.8 cm) slit along the fold line from the top, as indicated on the pattern. Thread the needle with black thread, and sew the top, slanted edges (the shoulders) together using a blanket stitch (see page 114).

4. Fold the two arm pieces in half along the dotted lines. Blanket-stitch along the top and side edges that are joined.

5. Slide each of the arms, folded side on the bottom, just inside the top edges of the body's side seams (at the end of the seams that you've just sewn). Blanket-stitch them in place along the lines of the side seams on both the front and the back. (Do not sew all the way through the two thicknesses of the body, or you won't be able to manipulate the rabbit's arms later with your fingers.) On the unfolded edge of the body, blanket-stitch the edges together.

6. To make the head, use white thread to sew up the pattern's darts on the wrong side of the front of the head. Place the front and back of the head together with wrong sides facing, and blanket stitch around them, leaving the bottom edge open for stuffing later. Sew two black beads into place for the eyes, and three purple beads in an inverted triangle for the nose. Use a small line of straight stitches to outline the rabbit's mouth.

7. To make the ears, fold the two pieces along the pattern's dotted lines. Blanket-stitch the edges with black thread. Fold the bottom edges of each ear together, and attach them along the pattern's lines on the back of the head with the stitched sides facing front. Stuff the head with fiberfill or cotton, then slide the bottom edges of it inside the neck, or top edge, of the body. Blanket-stitch the head in place with black thread across the front and the back. (Again, do this on both sides, not through two thicknesses, so that you can put fingers in the head later.)

8. Cut a small strip of red felt that measures 1½

inches (3.75 cm) by ½ inch (12.5 cm) for use as the bow. Tack the bow into place with thread at the seam where the neck joins the body. Sew the button into place underneath the bow.

9. Place the felt-covered yogurt container upside down on the piece of cardboard. Trace around the edge with the pen, and remove it. Draw another circle ⅛-inch (3 mm) inside this circle with a pen and compass. Then add another circle that is an inch (2.5 cm) larger in diameter than this circle. Cut the brim out along the lines of the added circles.

10. Trace the brim twice onto the paper side of the black, adhesive-backed felt. Cut out the felt pieces, adding about ¼ inch (6 mm) to each edge. Peel the backing off, and cover both sides of the brim with them, lapping the excess felt over to cover the edges. Cut small slits with the craft knife about ¼ inch (6 mm) in from the inside edges of the brim on either side for inserting the black elastic cord. Place the brim on top of the felt-covered yogurt container, and fold the extra felt inside.

11. Use the craft knife to cut two small slits that line up with the slits in the brim about ½ inch (1.3 cm) down from the edges of the yogurt container. Tie a knot in the end of the black elastic, and push the other end from the inside of the slit out, and up through the corresponding brim slit. Then thread the elastic down through the slits on the other side of the hat. Tie the cord off on the inside of the hat to secure it.

12. Cut a strip of red, adhesive-backed felt that measures 3 inches (7.5 cm) wide by 12 inches (30 cm) long (or the top inside circumference of your hat). Begin peeling off the felt's paper backing, and position it along the upper edge of the hat over the inside, overlapping edge of the brim. Press it in place, making sure that you hold the edges of the brim in place with it.

13. Pull the rabbit up through the other end of the hat (normally the top) until the hem of the rabbit meets the edge. Cut a strip of black, adhesive-backed

Rabbit, *continued*

felt that measures 2 inches (5 cm) wide by 11 inches (27.5 cm) long (or the bottom inside circumference of your hat). Secure the rabbit to the inside of the hat with this piece by placing it about ¼ inch (6 mm) up along the outside edge of the hat before pulling it around to the inside where you overlap the hem and inside of the rabbit.

14. Use a pen to trace the letters that spell ABRACADABRA in reverse on the yellow felt (flip the stencil over so that the front side is on the felt). Cut out the letters, then use fabric glue to glue them right side up onto the face of the hat. (Divide the word into several phrases, and stack the letters in three rows from the top of the hat down to the brim. When you turn the hat over, the letters will be upside down.)

15. Push your hand up through the bottom of the hat, and place your thumb and outside finger inside the arms of the rabbit. Stick your forefinger inside the head of the rabbit. To hide the rabbit, pull him back down into the hat.

Radiant Sun Face

Blast away the blues with this freestanding decoration for your office or home.

DESIGNED BY
DEE DEE TRIPLETT

You Will Need

- 15 × 30-inch (37.5 × 75 cm) piece of red felt for backing
- 9 × 12-inch (22.5 × 30 cm) felt pieces in the following colors: gold; salmon; light and dark orange; light, medium, and dark pink; red
- 2 yards (1.8 m) fusible web
- Copper metallic thread and orange thread to match face (optional)
- ¼-inch (6 mm) dowel, 16-inches long (40 cm)
- 3½-inch (8.8 cm) square scrap of wood
- Gold paint (for dowel)
- Pencil
- Iron
- Scissors
- Sewing machine (optional)
- Drill with ¼-inch (6 mm) bit

Instructions

1. Enlarge the patterns on page 120 to the size indicated. Trace pattern A onto the paper side of the fusible web. Iron the fusible web onto half of the 15 × 30-inch (37.5 × 75 cm) piece of red felt to create a shape on which to work. (Protect your ironing board with a piece of old cloth when using fusible web.) Cut the shape out, leaving the paper attached to the back. You'll be attaching the facial features and rays to the other side, and the paper will prevent the web from sticking to your ironing board.

2. Trace nine copies of pattern B (the ray) onto the paper side of the fusible web. Cut out each of the rays in a rectangular piece, leaving room to iron each onto a piece of felt. Fuse one to the end of each 9 × 12-inch (22.5 × 30 cm) felt piece.

3. Cut out each of the rays, then cut each along the inner lines of the pattern to create three separate sections. Set these pieces aside.

4. Trace patterns C and D (round face with eyeholes and circle) onto the paper side of the fusible web. Fuse the circle pattern to a piece of the medium pink felt, and the round face with eyeholes to a piece of dark orange felt. Cut the shapes out, including the eyeholes. Remove the paper from the back of the dark orange piece, and leave it intact on the medium pink piece.

5. Use patterns E-H to trace and cut the facial features as follows: two eyeballs of dark hot pink, one forehead/nose of gold, two cheeks of salmon, and lips of medium pink. Remove fusible paper from all these pieces.

6. Place the medium pink circle, paper side down, on your ironing board. Position the eyeballs under the eyeholes of the dark orange face. Iron both in place on top of the hot pink circle. Repeat this process with the rest of the features to form a completed sun face.

7. Place the red felt sun that you cut out in step 1 paper-side-down on the ironing board. Mix up the different-colored ray shapes that you cut earlier, and arrange them in various combinations of your choice atop the red piece. Iron them onto the base.

8. Now fuse the completed face to the base. (You can further embellish the piece by machine sewing over the rays with metallic thread, and around the eyeholes and the nose with orange thread, but this step is optional.)

9. Paint the dowel with gold paint, and allow it to dry.

10. Remove the paper backing from the back of the red base. Place the finished piece atop the other half of the red felt that you cut in step 1. Position the dowel between the layers, and fuse the layers together.

Sun Face, *continued*

11. Remove the dowel. Trim the edges of the sun to create a matching back piece. Machine sew close to the edge of the sun's face, leaving the hole open on the edge for the dowel.

12. To make a wooden base, drill a ¼-inch (6 mm) hole in the center of the scrap of wood. To cover the base, cut out three pieces of fusible web that fit the wooden piece: two rectangles for two of the sides, and one large rectangle that will fit over the top and the connecting sides. Fuse the web to your leftover felt scraps, remove the paper, and fuse the pieces to the wood with the iron. (Fusible web works on wood as well as fabric.) Use the same process to cut decorative triangles and diamonds from felt to add as a final embellishment. Insert the dowel into the base, and let the sun shine!

Pet Mobile

DESIGNED BY
GAY D. FAY KELLY

Pet portraits adorn this movement-filled mobile. Use our patterns, or make up your own rendition of your family's pets to bob playfully from a ceiling.

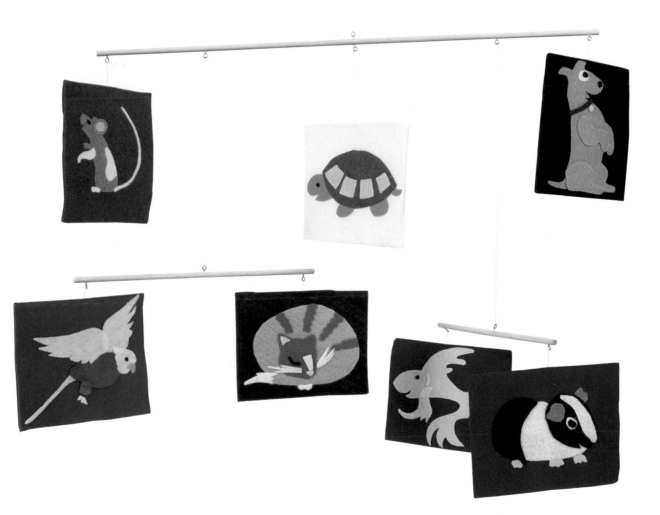

You Will Need

- 2 panels of red, blue, lavender, purple, green, yellow, and orange felt, 5 × 6 inches (12.5 × 15 cm) each
- Scraps of felt in white, black, blue, tan, gold, orange, light green, dark green, brown, and pink
- Monofilament fishing line
- 4-foot-long (1.2 m) piece of 3/16-inch (5 mm) wooden dowel

- 12 small, brass screw eyes
- Clear fingernail polish
- Fabric glue or iron-on adhesive
- Iron, if using iron-on adhesive
- Appliqué scissors, or other small, pointed scissors
- Fine-toothed saw
- Pushpin

Instructions

1. Enlarge the patterns on page 121 to size indicated. If using glue to attach the pet designs, use the patterns provided to cut out felt in the colors of your choice, using the pictures as a guideline for each animal. If using iron-on adhesive, trace the patterns onto the adhesive paper backing. Cut loosely around each of the

shapes, adding at least a ¼-inch (6 mm) margin. Iron the shapes onto the appropriate colors, then cut out the designs.

2. Choose from one of the following methods for attaching the designs:

   a. If using fabric glue, glue each of the animals in position on one of the 5 × 6-inch (12.5 × 15 cm) panels. (The mouse goes on a lavender panel, the cat on a green panel, the bird on an orange panel, the fish on a blue panel, the dog on a purple

panel, the turtle on a yellow panel, and the guinea pig on a red panel.)

   b. If using iron-on adhesive, follow the manufacturer's instructions and attach the pieces to each rectangle. Where layers of felt are thick, it may be necessary to iron both sides of the felt

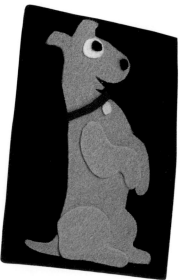

for complete adhesion. Use fabric glue on the edges if needed.

3. Cut 1 yard (90 cm) of monofilament for hanging each of the panels. Tie a 2- to 3-inch (5-7.5 cm) loop in the end of each. Apply glue to the blank, undecorated panels, and place a loop on top of each. Position the matching, decorated felt square on top, sandwiching the monofilament between the two pieces of felt. Allow to dry, then inspect and reglue where necessary.

4. Cut a 21-inch (52.5 cm) piece of dowel. Make a

small hole with the pushpin at its midpoint, and screw in a screweye. On the opposite side, make five holes with the pushpin and attach screweyes: two that are each ¼ inch (6 mm) from each end, two that are each 4½ inches (11.3 cm)

from each end, and one in the middle opposite the first screweye you inserted.

5. Cut two 11-inch (27.5 cm) pieces of dowel. Attach two screw eyes in each dowel, ½ inch (1.3 cm) from each end. Attach one in the middle of each dowel, on the opposite side.

6. Use a clove hitch and two half hitches to knot the monofilament to the screw eye of the 21-inch

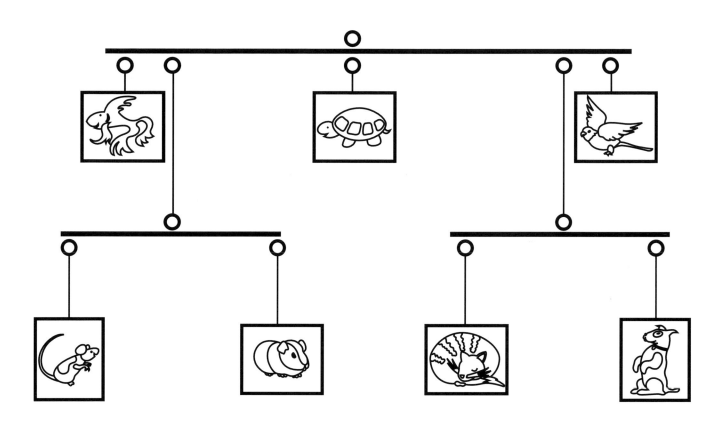

(52.5 cm) dowel. Secure the knots with a dab of clear fingernail polish. Use monofilament to hang the dowel at a height convenient for adjusting the balance of the mobile. Referring to the figure above, hang the turtle in the center of this dowel, using the same knotting technique. Then hang the

other two dowels and their panels as designated, balancing them as you shorten or lengthen the monofilament. Make sure there is clearance for all panels to move freely. When you're done and the nail polish is dry, trim any monofilament ends. Hang your mobile, being sure that small children cannot reach the monofilament.

Dogs-on-Holiday Scarves

Outfit your dog for any special day with an easy-to-make dog scarf. Use our patterns, or make up your own. Fido will be eternally grateful for the extra attention he'll receive!

DESIGNED BY
HOLLY DECKER

You Will Need

- 1 yard (90 cm) each of green, red, and black felt
- Cloth tape measure
- Piece of white felt and navy blue felt, each 9 × 12 inches (22.5 × 30 cm)
- 9 × 12-inch (22.5 × 30 cm) piece of orange felt
- Scissors
- Fabric glue
- American flag embroidered patch (pre-sewn)

Instructions

1. To make the three scarves shown, cut out identical pieces from the green, red, and black felt that approximate the measurements shown at right. (This scarf was created for a medium-sized dog. If your dog is larger or smaller you can reduce or enlarge the size of the scarf to fit.)

2. Enlarge the patterns on page 120 to size indicated, and cut out the pumpkin from the orange felt, the candy cane from the red felt, the candy cane's stripes from the white felt, and the stars from the blue and the white felt.

3. Smear glue on the back of the pumpkin, and press it in place in the center of the black scarf. Make sure to put glue around all of the edges so that it won't peel back while your dog is wearing it.

4. Repeat this process for attaching the candy cane and its stripes to the green felt scarf, and the stars to the red felt scarf. Glue a flag patch to the center of the red scarf.

2 inches (5 cm)

24 inches (62 cm)

9 inches (23 cm)

18 inches (46 cm)

24 inches (62 cm)

2 inches (5 cm)

Fat Cat Mat

DESIGNED BY
CAROLYNN WILLIAMS

Preserve that antique chair seat that your cat Buster stubbornly adorns, no matter how many times you plead with him. Make him a cat mat that will please both of you. Even though he won't ACT grateful, he'll graciously deposit hairs on this washable, attractive mat.

You Will Need

- ¼ yard (22.5 cm) white felt, 36 inches (90 cm) wide
- ¾ yard (67.5 cm) dark red felt, 36 inches (90 cm) wide
- 2 pieces of denim-blue felt, each 9 × 12 inches (22.5 × 30 cm)
- 1 piece of gray felt, 9 × 12 inches (22.5 × 30 cm)
- ⅝ yard (55.8 cm) iron-on fleece
- Spools of white, red, and blue sewing thread to match felt colors
- Transparent nylon thread
- 1 skein of gold rayon embroidery floss
- 1 skein of black rayon embroidery floss
- Rotary cutter and mat
- Sewing/craft ruler
- Sewing machine
- Appliqué needle
- Embroidery needle
- Iron
- Scissors
- Purple vanishing ink fabric marker

Before you begin, please note:

- All seams are ¼ inch (6 mm) wide.
- Add a ¼-inch (6 mm) seam allowance on all sides when cutting patterns A, B, and C

Instructions

1. Enlarge the patterns on page 121 to the size indicated.

2. Cut the following from the felt colors indicated:
FROM WHITE FELT, CUT:
- Six 4½-inch (11.3 cm) squares
- Two 4⅞-inch (12.2 cm) squares, cut in half diagonally
- Two of pattern A with seam allowance
- One of pattern B with seam allowance
FROM DENIM-BLUE FELT, CUT:
- Two 4⅞-inch (12.2 cm) squares, cut in half diagonally
- One 2⅞-inch (7.2 cm) square, cut in half diagonally (ears)
- One 3¹¹⁄₁₆-inch (9.2 cm) square, cut in half diagonally (face)

- Two of pattern C with seam allowance
FROM DARK RED FELT, CUT:
- One 20½-inch (51.3 cm) square (back of mat)
- Four 2½ × 20½-inch (6.3 × 51.3 cm) strips (borders)
- Two 4⅞-inch (12.2 cm) squares, cut in half diagonally
- One 3¹¹⁄₁₆-inch (9.2 cm) square, cut in half diagonally (face)
- One of pattern D (tail)
FROM IRON-ON FLEECE, CUT:
- Two 19½-inch (48.75 cm) squares

3. Place a denim-blue triangle and a dark red triangle right sides together. Machine sew a ¼-inch (6 mm) seam along the long edge to form a square when the piece is opened out. Repeat. Then sew a white triangle to a blue triangle to form a square of the same size, and repeat. Use the same process to make a square from a white triangle and a red triangle. Repeat.

4. Iron all of the squares and check their sizes. They should all measure 4½ inches (11.3 cm).

5. Using the lower left quadrant of the finished piece as a guide, sew together four of these six squares to form a larger square (see figure at right as a guide to the colors). To do this, place the right sides of two of the squares together, and sew a ¼-inch (6 mm)

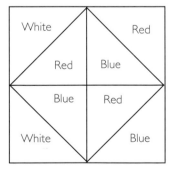

seam along the edge (make sure to position them correctly, according to the diagram.) Repeat this for the other two squares. Press them out with an iron, then put the right sides of these two long rectangles together, and sew up the long seam so that they form a big square.

Cat Mat, *continued*

6. Place the long edge of one of the smaller blue triangles (cut from a 2⅞-inch [7.2 cm] square) along the edge of one of the diagonally cut sides of pattern B. Sew it in place with a ¼-inch (6 mm) seam. Repeat with the other blue triangle. When opened out, the piece forms a 4½-inch (11.3 cm) square.

7. Sew the two blue and two white triangles cut from patterns A and C together to form an 8½ x 4½-inch (21.3 x 11.3 cm) rectangle that will form the cat's breast, as seen at right.

8. To make the patterned square for the cat's face, cut the dark red and denim-blue triangles that you cut from the 3¹¹⁄₁₆-inch (9.2 cm) squares in half again. Sew together the pieces with ¼-inch (6 mm) seams (see figure at left).

9. Refer to the photo of the finished piece, and sew all of the blocks remaining unsewn into vertical rows, press the back with an iron, then sew the rows together.

10. Align the edges of the dark red border strips with the edges of the face of the quilt. Sew them into place with a ¼-inch (6 mm) seam. Flip them out, and miter the corners of the strips (or sew them together at an angle).

11. In preparation for appliquéing the tail to the piece, carefully remove about 1½ inches (3.8 cm) of stitching from the seam between the dark red triangle and the white triangle where the tail joins the back of the cat (see finished piece). Tuck about ¼ inch (6 mm) of the tail between the red and the white triangle. Using red sewing thread and a needle, resew the seam by hand,

catching the end of the tail. Appliqué the rest of the tail in place with small stitches.

12. Using the vanishing ink marker, delineate the eyes, nose, and whiskers on the square for the cat's face, using pattern E as a guide. Use black and gold rayon embroidery floss (two strands) to embroider the cat's eyes, nose, and whiskers as shown on the pattern.

13. Center and iron the fleece to the wrong side of the quilted front and the red back. (The fleece is cut smaller to lessen the bulk of the seams.)

14. With right sides together, sew the mat together with a ¼-inch (6 mm) seam, leaving approximately 8 inches (20 cm) on one edge open. Turn the mat right side out, and slipstitch the opening shut.

15. Using the nylon thread in the sewing machine and bobbin, stitch in the ditch of all the patches to quilt the two pieces together.

16. Using the vanishing marker and patterns to trace an outline of the mouse's head, two paws, and tail on the gray felt. Cut out all of the above pieces. Appliqué them in place on the bottom right corner of the mat. Then mark the features and whiskers on the head with the marker before embroidering them with a strand of black embroidery floss and a stem stitch.

Frog Slippers

What excuse do you need to have this much fun? These hilarious slippers will gather giggles from everyone around. They're designed to fit a medium child's foot, or a small adult's foot.

You Will Need

- ⅔ yard (59.4 cm) embossed green felt or plain green felt
- 12-inch (30 x 30) square of off-white felt
- 9 x 12-inch (22.5 x 30 cm) piece of purple felt
- Scrap of white felt and red felt
- Off-white sewing thread
- Green sewing thread
- Sewing needle

- 12-inch (30 x 30 cm) square of non-skid rug backing or thin suede leather
- Bag of polyester fiberfill
- Scissors
- Fabric glue
- Sewing machine

DESIGNED BY
MONA-KATRI MAKELA

Instructions for Frog Slippers

1. Enlarge the patterns on page 122 to the size indicated, and cut out the felt pieces as described on them.

2. Place the right side of one of the heels of the inner slipper lining and the back of one of the sides of the lining together. Machine sew them together with a narrow seam. In the same fashion, sew the other side of the inner lining to the heel on the opposite side. Then sew together the curved edges (toe portion) of the sides of the lining. Repeat this process to create the second lining.

3. With right sides together, sew the soles to the bottoms of the linings along the edge.

4. With right sides together, sew the top and bottom pieces for the back and the front legs together with a narrow seam, gathering the curves as needed. Turn the sewn legs right side out.

5. With right sides together, sew each of the nose/forehead pieces to the sides of the slippers between the stars on the pattern. Repeat this process to sew the other side pieces to the nose/forehead on the opposite side.

6. Sew the heels of the slippers to the back edges of the sides of the slippers with right sides together. (You should have a closed form at this point that represents the frog's body minus the legs and eyes.) Repeat this process with the same pieces for the second slipper. Do not turn these pieces out yet.

7. Stuff the green slipper tops into the linings, aligning the top edges of both by centering the heel on the back. (The inside or right sides of the lining will be facing the right sides of the top of the slipper.)

8. Sew the top edge of the two pieces together, then pull the top part of the slipper (or frog's body) back out. Pull it down around the slipper.

9. Hand sew the sides of each sole (between the dots on the pattern) to each of the bottom edges of the body of the slipper, leaving the heel and toe open for stuffing.

10. Use the polyester fiberfill to stuff the rear and sides of each slipper through the heel opening. Before stuffing the top, insert your feet into the slippers. Then add enough fiberfill through the toe opening to comfortably fill the slippers until they're snug on your feet. Sew up the sole's heel and toe openings by hand.

11. Stuff each of the legs with fiberfill. Use a blanket stitch (see page 114) to hand sew the edges of the legs in place on the body of the piece. (Use the pattern as a guide for positioning them.)

12. To make the eyes, sew long gathering stitches around the edges of each of the purple felt circles, then pull up the threads to make a pouch. Stuff each pouch with fiberfill before tightening it until it is closed. Hand sew each of the openings closed. Sew the pouches onto the body of each frog, using the pattern notation as a guide for placement. Cut four small circles of white felt for the eye centers, and glue them in place with fabric glue. Use a black marker to make a dot in the center of each eye.

13. Glue on the pieces that form the frog's mouth on either side of the tip of the nose, beginning each at the seam between the top and side pieces.

14. Cut a pair of soles out of the non-skid rug backing. Use fabric glue to attach them to the felt soles that you've already sewn in place.

Jester's Stocking

This playful, witty stocking is really easy to make. You don't have to be an experienced sewer to complete this project.

You Will Need

- ½ yard (45 cm) red felt
- Small pieces of red, yellow, and green felt, measuring at least 8 × 5 inches (20 × 12.5 cm) each
- A dozen red, yellow, and green buttons in various shapes, sizes, and designs
- 2 yards (1.8 m) each of ⅛-inch (3 mm) red and green ribbon
- 2 yards (1.8 m) of ½-inch (1.3 mm) yellow ribbon
- Straight pins
- Hand sewing needle or sewing machine
- Red sewing thread
- Scissors

DESIGNED BY
MARY D'ALTON

Instructions

1. Enlarge the pattern on page 123 to the size indicated, and cut out two identical stocking pieces from the red felt. Stitch the two pieces together by hand or machine.

2. From the small piece of red felt, cut a rectangle out of each that measures 8 × 3½ inches (20 × 8.8 cm). From the yellow and green felt pieces, cut a rectangle that measures 8 × 4½ inches (20 × 11.3 cm).

3. Cut the lower edges of the rectangles with uneven, jagged patterns, varying each. Overlap them at the top of the stocking: red on top, green in the middle, and yellow last. Arrange the pieces until you're pleased with the way they look, then pin them in place.

4. Along the top edge of the yellow piece, use a loose stitch to attach it to the front of the stocking by

hand. Add the green piece in the same fashion. Sew the red piece to the top with stitches that are whipped from behind the stocking's top edge.

5. Arrange your selection of buttons randomly on top of the layers that you've created, and sew them in place. Place a larger one in the upper right corner of the stocking.

6. Fold the ribbons in half to form a loop. Stitch them together by hand about 2 inches (5 cm) from the fold. At the point where you joined them into a bundle, stitch them in place behind the big button. Finish the stocking by trimming the ends of the ribbons to different lengths of your choice.

Perky Parrot Costume

Believe it or not, this is an idea born of a last-minute need for a child's costume. This designer/mom took a hooded sweatshirt, and sewed on pieces of colorful felt for feathers until she had a full bird. Loads of fun!

DESIGNED BY
MARY D'ALTON

You Will Need

- Hooded sweatshirt with zip-up front in size that fits child snugly
- Pieces of brightly colored, washable felt in colors of your choice that add up to about 2 yards (1.8 m) of felt
- Fabric marker
- Straight pins
- Scissors
- Sewing machine with thread

Instructions

1. Enlarge the patterns on pages 124 and 125 to the size indicated, and make multiple photocopies of the patterns that are combined in layers (such as those that form the crest of the bird's head).

2. Cut the patterns out of paper, making certain that you cut one for each of the pieces indicated. Use the fabric marker to trace the crest patterns onto various colors of felt. Cut out the pieces, and then reassemble them one on top of the other as they are configured in the original pattern.

3. Use the patterns to cut out the tail plumes in the same manner. Reassemble them on a flat surface so that you won't be confused later.

4. Follow the same procedure to cut out one set of sleeve patterns from various colors of felt, and reassemble them. Then reverse the pattern pieces (or flip them over), mark them on felt, and cut out a second set of of pieces for the opposite sleeve. Follow

this same procedure to cut out the pieces that fit onto the side of the hood.

5. Now that you've cut out your key pieces, sew them into place first. To sew the crest into place, pin the pieces on in layers that mimic the original pattern. Sew each piece into place with your machine by running a stitch about ¼ inch (6 mm) from each straight edge. (Begin with the bottom pieces first, and then add the top. Add the last, crowning piece by sewing a t-shape at the center through all of the layers.)

6. Add the layers that make up the feathers on either side of the hood underneath the crest using the same guidelines. Attach both sets of sleeve feathers in the same way, paying attention the the fact that the longer feathers go in the back.

7. To add the tail plumes, line up the straight edges of the pieces, and sew the three layers together on the top about 2 inches (5 cm) inside the edge of the top piece. Attach the plumes near the bottom edge of the hood in the center.

8. Use patterns A, B, and C to cut out felt pieces in contrasting colors, and pin them into place in layers in the open portions of the sweatshirt. (Begin by using pattern D along the inside edges next to the zipper, pattern C to fill in big areas on the back, and patterns A and B to fill in gaps underneath the arms and between pieces.)

9. Keep adding layers of feathers until you are satisfied with your bird.

Daffodil Plant Pokes

These cheerful flowers will brighten even the most daunting of days. The following materials and instructions are for making a dozen daffodils.

You Will Need

- ¼ yard (22.5 cm) each of the following felts: bright yellow, yellow-orange, white, bright green
- 12 wooden dowels, each ¼ inch (6 mm) wide, 12 inches (30 cm) long
- Wide-tipped green permanent marker
- Sharp pencil
- Fabric glue
- Scissors
- Purple vanishing ink marker

Instructions

1. Color each of the dowels with the green marker, and set them aside to dry.

2. Enlarge the patterns on page 125 to the size indicated.

3. Cut out the patterns. Use the vanishing ink marker to trace 12 sets of leaves and 12 flower backs onto the green felt. Cut them out.

4. Trace 12 trumpets and flower bases onto the white, bright yellow, and yellow-orange felt. (Vary the colors so that you'll end up with a mixed bouquet of colors.) Cut out all of the pieces.

5. Cut slits in the centers of the flower bases where they're indicated on the pattern. Be careful not to cut all the way to the edges.

6. Fold the outside point of each flower petal in towards the center of the flower. Pull each petal back through the slit that you've cut at its base. (Pull very gently so that you won't rip the felt.)

DESIGNED BY
TERRY ALBRIGHT

7. Lay each flower face down with the back up. (The back will have a sunken inner circle.) Use fabric glue to attach the top of each of the dowels to the backs of the flowers.

8. Glue each of the flower backs, or green felt circles, over the exposed dowel, covering the center of the back.

9. Cut slits along one edge in the trumpet portions of the flowers as indicated on the pattern. Run a bead of glue along the uncut long edge of each of the trumpets, and tightly roll up each.

10. Glue a trumpet on the front of each flower. Use your fingers to lightly separate the fringed edges.

11. Run a bead of glue along the bottom straight edge of each set of leaves. Wrap the piece around the dowel at a midway point. Hold the base of the leaves tightly in place until the glue sets.

12. Place your flowers in a vase, or stick them in a long planter full of border grass.

Floral Table Mat

Layer a colorful group of flowers and leaves around the edges of a piece of cut felt, and *voila!*—you've got a charming mat to adorn the center of your table.

You Will Need

- 1 yard (90 cm) dark green felt
- 9 × 12-inch (22.5 × 30 cm) felt squares in each of the following colors: red, gold, baby blue, medium blue, bright blue, turquoise, light pink, hot pink, white, bright green, dark green
- 3 skeins of black, 6-ply embroidery floss
- Purple vanishing ink fabric marker
- Scissors
- Round dinner plate
- Fabric marker pen or chalk
- Straight pins
- Embroidery needle
- Fabric glue
- ½-inch-wide (1.3 cm) flat paintbrush

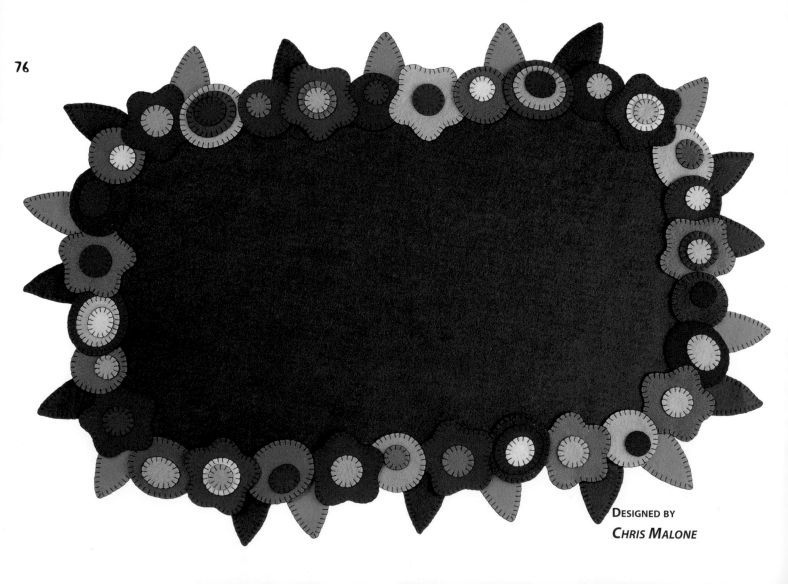

DESIGNED BY
CHRIS MALONE

Instructions

1. Cut a 15 × 24-inch (37.5 × 60 in) rectangle from the dark green felt. Fold the felt in half crosswise, matching the edges.

2. Use the dinner plate as a guide to mark a curved line with the chalk or marker pen at each of the four corners. Trim along these lines through both layers. Unfold the felt piece.

3. Enlarge the patterns for the flowers and leaves on page 125 to the size indicated, and cut them out.

4. Use the vanishing ink marker to trace flower shapes (petal, round, and oval) and leaves onto the swatches of colored felt. (Vary the colors so that you can play with the shapes as you place them out around the perimeter of the mat.) Cut out the shapes. You can add more later as you need them.

(**Note:** Our mat has 31 flowers: 12 petal-shaped, 10 round, and 9 oval. Most of the flowers have a single center; eight have two centers. We've used 21 leaves composed of 11 dark green and 10 light green.)

5. Thread the embroidery needle with two strands of black embroidery floss, and attach the round center to each flower with buttonhole stitches (see page 114). Create stitches that are approximately ³⁄₁₆ inch

(5 mm) long and ³⁄₁₆ inch (5 mm) apart. Edge all of the leaves and the edges of the flowers with the same stitch.

6. Arrange the completed flowers around the outside border of the table mat, overlapping them and allowing about one-third of each flower to hang over the mat's edge. Vary the color combinations and shapes. Colors that tend to stand out more, such as gold, red, and white, should be evenly distributed around the edge.

7. Insert leaves at intervals between the mat and the flowers. When you're satisfied with the arrangement, pin each flower and leaf in place.

8. Starting at any point on the mat, unpin a flower or leaf, squeeze out a thin coat of fabric glue, distribute it with the paintbrush on the back of the piece, and press it in place. (Be careful to apply glue only to the area where the flower or leaf will touch the mat.) Proceed around the mat in one direction, overlapping and gluing one piece after the other.

9. Place a weight, such as a stack of books, on each section of the mat while the glue is drying, to help facilitate bonding between the felt pieces. Allow the glue to dry thoroughly, and then glue edges as needed.

Woven Wool Felt Pillow

This unusual pillow is made by weaving strips of felt in and out of the face of the pillow. A fun project for kids to try!

You Will Need

- 22 × 22-inch (55 × 55 cm) foam pillow form
- 1⅓ yards (1.2 m) black wool felt
- 8 × 36-inch (20 × 90 cm) strips of wool felt in the following colors: red, orange, yellow, purple, olive green, bright green, tan
- ½ yard (1.3 m) 36-inch-wide (90 cm) bright green felt (for piping)

DESIGNED BY
LISA VIVEIROS

- 2¾ yards (6.9 cm) 1-inch-thick (2.5 cm) cotton piping
- White marking pencil
- Rotary cutter with scalloped-edge blade
- Pinking shears
- Scissors
- Paper and pencil
- Black thread
- Sewing needle
- Clothing dryer
- Sewing machine

Instructions

1. Hand wash and tumble dry the orange and red strips of 8 × 36 inch (20 × 90 cm) felt. (Do each individually to avoid bleeding.) The wool will shrink when washed and dried.

2. Use the rotary cutter and mat to cut the felt strips as follows: cut the olive green into 1-inch (2.5 cm) strips for the leaves, cut the tan into ¾-inch (1.9 cm) strips for the stems, and cut the other colors into a variety of widths ranging loosely from ¾ to 1½ inches (1.9 × 3.8 cm). Cut a variety of pinked and straight edges.

3. Cut out two 23-inch (57.5 cm) squares from the black wool felt.

4. Use a white marking pencil and the figure at the right as a guide to sketch the positions of the stems and flowers on one of the black felt squares. Then make slits in the felt that are approximately ½ inch (1.3 cm) wide at the beginning and end of each of the dotted lines. (You'll be weaving the felt up through one of the slits, over the top of the pillow, and then back down through the next slit.)

5. Begin by weaving the center stem with the tan strips. Pull one of the tan strips up through the bottom slit of the stem, from back to front. Leave a 3-inch-long (7.5 cm) tail for tacking the strip later. Twist the felt slightly, and then push it back through the next slit to the back. Come back to the front through the adjacent slit, twist again, and then push back through to the underside. Continue this weaving process until you've reached the top of this stem. After you've pushed through the final hole to the back, leave a 3-inch-long (7.5 cm) tail for tacking later. Use the same process to add the other branches of your stem by pushing tan felt strips up through several of the slits that you've already filled with the main part of the stem. Keep branching the stem in this fashion.

6. Add the dark green leaves next. Join each leaf with a stem by clipping two coordinating slits in the tan stem and the black pillow face. Pull up a short strip of dark green felt through the face and stem, and leave a tail. Push it back through a slit cut in the black felt that positions the leaf so that it fans out from the stem.

7. To form the flowers and buds you'll use similar weaving techniques. To make a flower like the floppy, fringed green that you see on the pillow, cut a series of small slits in rows on the pillow top. (We used six rows with four slits in each row about ½ inch (1.3 cm) apart.) Then cut narrow strips of green felt (pink the edges if you like) that are about ½ inch (1.3 cm) wide and 7 inches (17.5 cm) long. Pull both ends of each strip up through two adjacent holes, and knot the strip to form a tassel. Keep adding strips until you've made a fringed flower.

79

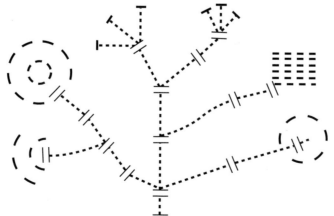

8. To make a flower like the purple one, use the same weaving technique that you used for making the leaves (simply pull the felt strip up through the pillow top and back under to form each petal). Weave with an extra-wide strip of at least 2 inches (5 cm) that has pinked edges to make a full-bodied flower.

9. For the orange flower, we used a variation on this idea. Once the strip is woven up and then under, bring the tail of it back through a slit cut ½ inch (1.3 cm) out from the previous one. Tie off the end of the tail close to the black felt on the face of the pillow. Then fringe the ends by cutting several slits in the end of the tail.

10. To weave other flowers, follow the same basic technique that was used to make the leaves (up through one slit and back through the next) in a circular formation. Create a center for your flower with one leaf-like piece, then use the same technique to add petals in colors that radiate from this center piece. Use the red felt that you washed and shrank to make textural petals in this fashion.

11. After you've created your motif, and all of the tails of the strips are pulled to the back of the pillow, tack them down with needle and thread so that they won't pull out later.

12. Cut three 4 × 36-inch (10 × 90 cm) strips of bright green felt together to cover the cotton piping. Fold the felt over the piping, match the edges together, and then machine sew close to the piping to cover it, leaving a border of about ½ inch (1.3 cm) that will be used to attach the piping to the pillow.

13. Place the pillow back and the pillow front wrong sides together. Sandwich the piping between the two sides, matching the edges of the pillow and the piping. Use straight pins to hold the piping in place, if needed. Begin machine sewing at one corner, and continue around on three sides. Leave one side unsewn.

14. Turn the pillow inside out to reveal the piping and the floral motif. Insert the pillow form, and hand sew the final side closed with black thread.

Wine Bottle Bag

This bag is a charming gift idea to transform a simple bottle of juice or wine into a thoughtful present.

You Will Need

- 2 pieces of black felt, 9 × 12 inches (22.5 × 30 cm) each
- 9 × 12-inch (22.5 × 30 cm) piece of lavender felt
- 9 × 12-inch (22.5 × 30 cm) piece of orchid felt
- Scrap of leaf green embossed felt
- 24-inch-long (60 cm) piece of narrow black cording
- Fusible web
- Black thread
- Straight pins
- Sewing machine

Instructions

1. Cut the two black felt pieces into 6¾- × 12-inch (16.9 × 30 cm) rectangles, and place them together. Sew the sides and bottom together with a ¼-inch (6 mm) seam allowance to form a bag. Pinch the corners of the bag together at right angles to the seams you've just sewn. Sew a seam across the corners that is 1 inch (2.5 cm) from the corner. Trim off the corners below this seam. Turn the bag right side out.

2. Enlarge the pattern on page 125 to the size indicated. Transfer the appliqué pattern onto the paper side of the fusible web. Cut out the traced shapes just beyond the lines. Iron eight of the grapes onto the lavender felt, and eight onto the orchid felt. Iron the two leaves onto the green embossed felt. Cut out the shapes. When cool, remove the paper backing, and position the grapes and leaves on front of the bottle bag using the finished piece as a guide for their placement. Iron the appliqués in place. Using black thread, blanket-stitch (see page 114) around the edges of the leaves and grapes.

3. Tie knots in the ends of the black cording. Thread the sewing machine with black thread. Position the midpoint of the cord at the top of the bag about 1 inch (2.5 cm) from the top at the centerpoint of the back. Wrap it loosely around the bag so that the two ends hang down evenly in the front. Pin it in place. Beginning 1 inch (2.5 cm) down from the top of the bag at the front center, machine stitch over the cording with a zigzag that is wide enough to encase the cord, and leave it room to move within the confines of the stitching. Remove the pins as you approach them to avoid breaking your needle. Reinforce the beginning and end of the stitching. Don't pierce the cording with the needle while you're sewing it.

4. Insert a wine or juice bottle into the bag, and cinch the cording around the bottle. Knot and tie the bow.

DESIGNED BY BARBARA BRUNSON

Embroidered Napkin Ring and Place Mat

Use a simple blanket stitch to sew up these beautiful table accessories. They're worth the time it takes to make them!

DESIGNED BY
VIVIAN PERRITTS

You Will Need for Each Napkin Ring

- 3 × 8-inch (7.5 × 20 cm) piece of light green felt
- 4 × 8-inch (10 × 20 cm) piece of gold felt
- 3 × 3-inch (7.5 × 7.5 cm) square of dark red felt
- 2 × 2-inch (5 × 5 cm) square of yellow felt
- 1 skein each, 6-strand embroidery floss, in the following colors: loden green, peach, yellow, pink, orange
- 1/16 yard (1.5 mm) lightweight, iron-on adhesive
- Scissors
- Embroidery needle

Instructions

1. Enlarge the patterns on page 123 to the size indicated. Trace patterns A and B to the paper side of the iron-on adhesive.

2. Trim loosely around the patterns, and iron pattern A onto yellow felt and pattern B onto dark red felt. Cut out the pieces for the flower.

3. Remove the paper backing from the iron-on adhesive. Fuse the flower pieces to the center of the green strip of felt.

4. Trim away a ¾-inch (1.9 cm) seam inside both edges of the green strip. (When you reach the edge of a flower petal, cut around it, so that it appears that the green strip runs behind it.) Cut around both the top and bottom petals.

5. Blanket-stitch (see page 114) around the edge of the flower with three strands of pink, embroidery floss. Blanket-stitch around the gold center with three strands of orange floss. Make approximately 20 French knots (see page 114) in the center of flowers, half with three strands of peach floss, and half with three strands of yellow floss.

6. Cut the piece of gold felt in half lengthwise to form two pieces that are 2 × 8 inches (5 × 20 cm).

7. Center the green band on one of the gold bands, and fuse it on top of it with a strip of iron-on adhesive. Blanket-stitch with loden green floss along the edges of green felt.

8. Apply iron-on adhesive to the back of this piece, and fuse it to the second gold band. Blanket-stitch along the outside edges with loden green floss.

9. Overlap the ends of the piece about 1 inch (2.5 cm) in the back, and sew in place with a blanket stitch. On the inside of the ring, whip the other inside edge down with small stitches.

You Will Need for Each Place Mat

- 2 pieces gold felt, each 13½ × 17 inches (33.8 × 42.5 cm)
- 2-inch (5 × 5 cm) square yellow felt
- 10½ × 14-inch (26.3 × 35 cm) piece of light green felt
- 3 × 7-inch (7.5 × 17.5 cm) piece of hot pink felt
- 3-inch (7.5 × 7.5 cm) square of dark red felt
- 2-inch (5 × 5 cm) square of dark purple felt
- 2-inch (5 × 5 cm) square of lavender felt
- 2-inch (5 × 5 cm) square of bright purple felt
- 2-inch (5 × 5 cm) square of light green felt
- 2 × 4-inch (5 × 10 cm) piece of dark green felt
- 1½-inch (3.8 × 3.8 cm) square of medium green felt
- 2 × 4-inch (5 × 10 cm) piece of pink felt
- 2-inch (5 × 5 cm) square of orange felt
- 1 skein each, 6-strand embroidery floss, in the following colors: loden green, pink, orange, peach, yellow, hot pink, dusty rose, dark green, medium blue, light green
- 1 yard (90 cm) lightweight, iron-on adhesive
- Embroidery needle

Instructions for Place Mat

1. Enlarge patterns A–J on page 123 to the size indicated.

2. Apply iron-on adhesive to the back of the 10½- x 14-inch (26.3 x 35 cm) piece of light green felt. Iron this piece on top of one of the 13½- x 17-inch (33.8 x 42.5 cm) pieces of gold felt leaving a 1½-inch (3.8 cm) border around the sides.

3. Edge the piece of green felt with a ¼-inch (6 mm) blanket stitch (see page 114) sewn with three strands of loden green floss.

4. Trace the flower and leaf patterns on the paper side of the iron-on adhesive. Cut out the shapes, leaving room around each. Apply each pattern to the color that is designated for it, using the photo on page 82 as a guide. Cut them out. Remove the paper backing, and fuse the pieces of felt to the place mat, using the photo as a reference for placement. Add the embroidery to the flowers, leaves, and stems. Blanket stitch around all leaf and flower parts. Chain stitch all stems. Stem stitch the centers of the leaves. Use French knots in the centers of flowers.

5. Apply iron-on adhesive to the back of the place mat. Fuse the place mat to the second 13½ x 17-inch (33.8 x 42.5 cm) piece of gold felt. Blanket-stitch with three strands of loden green floss around the place mat's edge.

84

Mosaic Felt Bottle

Transform an empty glass bottle with this lively pattern of felt pieces. This is a great project for kids.

You Will Need

- Glass bottle, vase, or jar of your choice
- Black, ultra-gloss glass paint
- 12-inch (30 cm) squares of white, dark green, bright green, light blue, and bright blue felt
- 1 sheet of double-sided adhesive
- 1-inch-wide (2.5 cm) paintbrush
- Pen
- Scissors

Instructions

1. Paint the glass form with two coats of black paint following the paint manufacturer's instructions for preparation, application, and drying times. Allow the paint to dry overnight.

2. Enlarge the patterns on page 123, and cut them out. (These patterns will be used to form the main design elements of the composition. The rest of the surface will be filled with randomly cut pieces of felt.)

3. To cover a medium-sized bottle, trace four of each flower pattern onto one side of the double-sided adhesive sheet, excluding the pattern marked with an X. Trace four outlines of the X pattern in a separate group. Group together and trace four outlines of each leaf on the double-sided adhesive.

3. Cut the repeated flowers, small leaves, and large leaves out of the adhesive sheet in separate sections.

4. Remove the unmarked side of the adhesive backing from each of the pattern sections. Adhere the smallest leaves to the dark green felt. Then cover a 2 by 2-inch (5 x 5 cm) section of the dark green felt with a blank square of adhesive, and save this for making felt stems later. Adhere the larger leaves to the bright green felt.

5. Press the flower patterns marked X to light blue felt, and the remaining flower sections to bright blue felt. Back half of the piece of white felt with a sheet of adhesive in preparation for cutting random mosaic shapes later.

6. Cut out the sections of the flowers one at a time along the lines that you traced on the adhesive backing. Peel away the backing on each and press it into place on the glass, using the original pattern as a guide for placement. Use a straight pin to lift the adhesive backing up if you have problems peeling it off. Vary the positions of the flowers as you place them around the sides of the vase. Add the leaves, placing them around and to the sides of the flowers.

7. For use as stems and vines, cut ⅛-inch-wide (3 mm) strips from the adhesive-backed dark green felt that you prepared earlier. Add stems of varying lengths to the flowers and leaves.

85

8. Cut small squares, rectangles, triangles, and strips from the white adhesive-backed felt. Use these pieces in a mosaic fashion to randomly fill in between the flowers and leaves.

DESIGNED BY
BARBARA MATTIESSEN

FLOWERS AND MORE

Wisteria Table Runner

This table runner is so stunning that you don't need any other decoration on your table. The variegated, hand-dyed, silk ribbon is custom made. The source that we used is listed on page 128.

You Will Need

- 1 piece of orchid purple felt, 36 inches (90 × 90 cm) square
- 1 piece of antique white felt, 36 inches (90 × 90 cm) square
- Lightweight fusible interfacing, 12 × 32 inches (30 × 81.3 cm)
- 1 skein of light green rayon floss
- 1 skein of off-white rayon floss
- 1 skein of purple rayon floss
- 16 yards (14.4 m) variegated purple, hand-dyed, 4 mm silk ribbon
- 7 yards (6.3 m) variegated green, hand-dyed, 4 mm silk ribbon
- Fabric glue
- Black marker
- Vanishing ink fabric marker
- White ink fabric marker
- Assortment of ribbon embroidery needles
- Pressure-sensitive rotary cutter
- Self-healing cutting mat
- Sewing/craft ruler
- Sharp scissors
- Iron

DESIGNED BY
TERRY ALBRIGHT

Instructions

1. Use the rotary cutter to cut pieces of antique white felt and fusible interfacing that each measure 15 × 32 inches (37.5 × 80 cm). Smooth the felt out with an iron on a low setting. Press the fusible interfacing to one side of the felt to stabilize it for stitching.

2. Enlarge the embroidery pattern on page 118 to the size indicated. Trace over the border and stitching lines with a black marker. For an easy method of transferring the large stitching pattern to one end of the white felt, tape the copied pattern to a window or light box, place the felt piece over it, and trace the lines with the vanishing ink marker (the ink from this pen will eventually evaporate and disappear). Turn the pattern around, and repeat this process on the other end. Then trace the border designs onto the center sides of the piece.

3. Thread a needle with two strands of the light green floss. Sew the lines that form the vines with a stem stitch. Cut the variegated green silk ribbon into 10-inch (25 cm) lengths for each group of leaves. Stitch the leaves with a ribbon stitch (see page 114).

4. For each of the wisteria bunches, cut two lengths of purple silk ribbon that are each 18 inches (45 cm) long. Thread an embroidery needle with the ribbon. Starting at the base of the cluster (where it attaches to the stem), sew very loose French knots (see page 114) with three wraps around the needle. Decrease the number of wraps around the needle and tighten the tension of the ribbon as you work your way down to the tip of the cluster.

5. Use a warm iron to press out any creases in the felt that formed during stitching. (Take care to avoid ironing over embroidered sections.) Use scissors to trim the outside edge of the white piece along the border lines that you traced earlier. Cut the straight edges with a rotary cutter. Remove any stitching marks by dabbing them with a cotton swab and water, or

allow them to disappear on their own with time.

6. Cut two pieces of orchid felt that measure 36 × 16 inches (90 × 40 cm) each. Iron out any creases.

7. Squeeze small dots of fabric glue about ½ inch (1.3 cm) from the edge on the wrong side of the white embroidered felt piece. (Do not glue the piece in the center area, or it will pucker.) Center the piece on the orchid felt, and press it into place.

8. Thread an embroidery needle with three strands of off-white floss, and use it to blanket-stitch the edge of the top piece to the purple felt piece.

9. Measure 1 inch (2.5 cm) out from the edge of the off-white piece, and mark a series of dots with the white ink pen. Using the dots as a guide, trim the orchid felt so that there is a 1-inch (2.5 cm) border of it left showing underneath the piece of white felt.

10. Glue the assembled piece onto the other orchid felt piece. Trim this piece of felt along the same lines as the top one. Thread the embroidery needle with four strands of purple floss. Blanket-stitch (see page 114) the two pieces of orchid felt together along the edge.

Sculpted Flower Pillow

This soft, plush pillow will draw even the most timid of visitors to sit beside you. It's irresistable!

You Will Need

DESIGNED BY
BARBARA MATTHIESSEN

- ½ yard (45 cm) of ivory plush felt
- ⅛ yard (8.8 cm) of dark green plush felt
- ⅛ yard (8.8 cm) of burgundy plush felt
- 14-inch-square (35 cm) pillow form
- Ivory sewing thread
- Fabric glue
- Scissors
- Fabric marker pen (optional)
- Sewing pins
- Sewing needle
- Sewing machine
- Pencil

Instructions

1. From the ivory felt, cut out two 15-inch-wide (37.5 cm) squares and one circle that is 2 inches (5 cm) in diameter.

2. Cut two long strips from the piece of dark green felt that are both 2 inches (5 cm) wide. Place the two pieces right sides together, and machine stitch a ⅜-inch (9 mm) seam to join one end of the strips. Trim the piece to a length of 64 inches (160 cm).

3. Enlarge the patterns on page 115 to the size indicated. Using the pattern for leaves, cut out six leaves from the dark green felt. Use the flower petal pattern to cut out two pieces from the burgundy felt. Use a fabric marker pen to trace and repeat the flower petal pattern 11 times, and cut out that piece as one unit.

4. Fold the long strip of dark green felt in half lengthwise, wrong sides together. Place the edges of the green strip together with those of the right side of one of the ivory squares. (Fold the strip toward the inside.) Begin pinning the strip around the square, matching the edges. As you round the corners of the square, gather the strip slightly and pin it. Trim and slip stitch the two ends of the strips together where they meet.

5. Machine stitch the green strip to the ivory square with a ⅜-inch (9 mm) seam.

6. Pin the second ivory square to this piece, right sides together. Stitch the squares together on three sides with a ½-inch (1.3 cm) seam (or just inside the other seam).

7. Trim the corners diagonally. Turn the pillow right side out and insert the pillow form. Slipstitch the remaining side closed.

8. Thread the sewing needle. Hand gather the straight edges of the three petal units with a loose, running stitch of double thread. Pull the threads up tight and knot. (Do not cut the thread.) Roll each petal unit into a tube, then secure with a couple of long stitches across the bottom edges. Secure the stitches with a knot, and trim the thread.

9. Run a loose stitch around the edge of the small ivory circle that you cut in step 1, and gather it. Pull the threads up tightly until the circle forms a fuzzy button for the center of the flower. Knot the thread and trim it.

10. Push the button into the center of the large flower. Stitch the center in place from underneath.

11. To curl the leaves and petals, first break the point from a pencil so that no lead is visible. Turn the leaves over. For each leaf, press the end of the pencil firmly onto one end, then drag the leaf from the other end while pressing the pencil into its center. Curl the ends of the petals with the same process.

12. Use fabric glue to attach the leaves and petals to the pillow. To create a ripple effect, compress the length of each leaf, and attach it where it meets the pillow. After gluing on the large flower, attach the smaller ones by hiding the ends under the edges of the leaves.

Primitive Vase Cozy

Nestle a vase filled with water and flowers inside of this unusual covering.

Designed by
Nancy Worrell

You Will Need

- 12 x 18-inch (30 x 45 cm) pieces of embossed, "snakeskin" felt in gold, black, and medium brown
- 4-inch (10 cm) square of piece black, embossed, "snakeskin" felt
- Skein of #5 black pearl cotton thread
- Black sewing thread
- Chenille needle
- Assortment of 15 wooden beads
- Sewing needle
- Scissors

Instructions

1. Enlarge the pattern on page 119 to the size indicated. For the sides of the vase, cut two gold pieces from pattern 1, two black from pattern 2, and two medium brown from pattern 3. Cut two bottom pieces out of black from pattern 4.

2. Thread the chenille needle with black pearl cotton thread. Place the three sets of strips back to back, and blanket-stitch (see page 114) each of them together at the edges.

3. To form the cozy, realign the strips to form a parallelogram. Join the two rows of blanket stitching on either side of each strip with black pearl cotton thread laced in and out of the two rows of blanket stitching.

4. Roll point C around to match D as indicated on the pattern. Continue with the same in and out stitch to begin spiraling up. Continue rolling and stitching until points A and B meet to form a cylinder.

5. To create the piece that will form the bottom of the cozy, use a blanket stitch to join the two pieces of black felt together, embossed sides out.

6. Align the bottom with one of the openings on the cylinder, and lace it in place.

7. Refer to the photograph of the final piece, and use the sewing needle and black sewing thread to tack beads to the black strip on the cozy.

Child's Throne

Use this beautiful, felt-upholstered throne as a decorative accent or doll's chair for a child's room. Personalize it with a monogram, and your child will truly feel royal.

You Will Need

- 1 cardboard throne (see suppliers' list on page 128)
- 3 yards (2.7 m) embossed felt for sides and back in color of your choice
- 2 yards (1.8 m) embossed felt for seat, back, and insides of rockers in color of your choice
- 4 to 5 yards (3.6 × 4.5 m) decorative embroidered ribbon, 1 inch (2.5 cm) wide
- 3 yards (2.7 m) flat, gold ribbon, ½ inch (1.3 cm) wide
- 6 yards (5.4 m) braided, gold cord/piping
- Pencil
- Vanishing ink fabric marker
- Fabric glue

Instructions

1. Fit the pieces of the throne together. After it is assembled, use a pencil to mark the lines where the sections of the throne join. (In other words, make marks that will tell you which areas of the cardboard will be covered after you've disassembled it.) While the throne is assembled, make decisions on which colors to use where. Make a color notation on the front, back, and sides so that you'll remember once it is taken apart again.

2. Disassemble the throne. Use the vanishing marker to trace one of the sides of the throne onto a piece of felt, omitting the areas that will be hidden behind a joint later (two layers of upholstery will add too much thickness when you rejoin the pieces). Repeat this process for the other sides and all areas that will be covered in felt, including the front and back. Cut out all of your pieces.

3. Turn one of the side upholstery pieces over, and squeeze glue on the wrong side around the edges. Then add random dots of glue over the rest of the surface. Place the cardboard piece flat on your working surface, and carefully position the felt upholstery on the piece. If it is slightly too large, leave it. It will be covered later with ribbon and braid. Continue to cover the chair with felt pieces in the same fashion until all of the surfaces are covered.

4. Trim all the facing edges on the front and sides with glued-on embroidered ribbon. Cover the outside facing edges of the bottom cross pieces with flat, gold ribbon.

5. As a final accent, add gold cord on either side of the ribbon that you've attached. (We completed our throne with a showy, criss-crossed, and knotted piece of cord on the front.)

DESIGNED BY
TANA BOERGER

Silk Ribbon Embroidery Box

Silk ribbon embroidery is really quite simple, but looks amazingly impressive. This box with embroidered flowers makes a lovely keepsake for years to come.

You Will Need

- ½ yard (75 cm) of embossed, floral-patterned maroon felt
- ½ yard (75 cm) of dark green silk ribbon, 4 mm wide
- 3 yards (2.7 m) of variegated pink silk ribbon, 4 mm wide
- 2 yards (1.8 m) of dark green rayon embroidery floss
- Papier-mâché or wooden box, 7 inches (17.5 cm) in diameter, 3 inches (7.5 cm) high
- Crewel embroidery stitching needle with large eye

- Pencil
- White vanishing ink marker
- Scissors
- Tailor's tracing paper
- Cloth measuring tape
- Fabric glue

DESIGNED BY
TERRY ALBRIGHT

Instructions

1. Use the white vanishing ink marker to trace an outline of the box lid on the right side of the maroon felt. (This mark will provide you with a boundary for your stitching.) Using this circle as a guide, cut the felt into a circle that is at least 8 inches (20 cm) in diameter.

2. Enlarge the embroidery pattern on page 118 to the size indicated and trace it onto tracing paper, or use a copy machine to copy it onto a piece of white paper. Cut out the circle and center it on the piece of felt. Slide a sheet of tailor's tracing paper between the pattern and the embossed side of the felt. Trace over the lines of the pattern with a pencil.

3. Thread the crewel embroidery needle with a four-ply strand of the dark green rayon embroidery floss. Beginning at the tip of each leaf, use the fly stitch (see page 114) to delineate the outlines of each of the three leaves. Tie off the end of each leaf on the underside of the felt, and trim the floss.

4. Thread a needle with a 12-inch (30 cm) length of pink variegated ribbon. Tie a knot in one end. Following the pattern, and beginning near the center of the design, come up through the back at the large base end of one of the flower bunches. To form the first third of the bunch, use the ribbon to form three-wrap French knots (see page 114). As you move toward the center of the bunch, taper the knots to two-wrap, ending with one-wrap knots at the tip of each bunch.

5. Thread a needle with a 12-inch (30 cm) length of dark green silk ribbon. Form the center of the design by making a flower-like configuration using straight stitches.

6. Apply glue to the top of the lid, making certain to place a line of glue near the edge. Center the piece on top of the lid, and press it into place, moving from the center of the lid out. When dry, apply glue to the sides of the lid, a little at a time, and then gently pull the felt down over the sides, smoothing it as you go. Trim any excess felt off along the lower edge with scissors. (Avoid wrapping the felt under the lid; it will create too much bulk for putting the lid on later.)

7. Cut a piece of maroon felt with a length which measures the circumference of the box, or 23 inches (57.5 cm). Cut the width of the piece to twice the height of the box, plus an inch, or 7 inches (17.5 cm). This piece will be used to cover the sides (both outside and inside) of the box.

8. Squeeze lines of fabric glue onto the back of the felt piece, paying special attention to the edges. Smear the glue slightly so that it won't drip while you're lining the box. Beginning on the inside of the box, position one of the long sides of the felt rectangle around the circumference of the box flush with the corner where the side meets the bottom. Overlap the edges that meet, tucking one under the other.

9. Pull the felt to the outside of the box, and continue to cover the box by pulling it down the outside wall. Press it neatly into place, continuing the seam overlap that you began on the inside. Tuck the excess felt around the bottom corner and onto the bottom of the box. Make sure that the edges are secured with glue.

10. Using the diameter of the inside of the bottom of the box as a guide, cut two circles of felt the same size, each 6½ inches (16.3 cm). Apply fabric glue to the backs of both pieces of felt, and press them into place on the inside bottom of the box and the outside bottom. (When you place the outside piece, you'll hide the edges of the felt that you wrapped onto the bottom of the box.)

Heart Memory Pins

U Use an old photo of your favorite relative to create a lasting thought to wear close to your heart.

You Will Need for Each Heart

▌ Two pieces mat board, each at least 3½ inches (8.8 cm) square

▌ 5-inch-square (12.5 cm) piece of felt in color of your choice

▌ 3-inch-square (7.5 cm) piece white or cream felt

▌ Iron-on photographic transfer film (you can buy this film for use on home scanners and ink-jet printers, or have the process done at a copy center)

▌ Small black and white photograph

▌ #5 pearl cotton embroidery thread in colors to coordinate with felt

▌ Sharp embroidery needle with large eye, or crewel embroidery needle

▌ Regular sewing needle

▌ Nymo beading thread

▌ Polyester fiberfill

▌ Beads and charms for embellishment

▌ Scissors

▌ Iron

▌ Craft knife

▌ White craft glue

▌ Jewelry pin back

For optional fringe:

▌ 32 seed beads

▌ 8 long tube beads

▌ 8 round beads, 10 mm

DESIGNED BY
BETTY AUTH

For tassel:

▌ 1 round bead, 8 mm

▌ 3 round beads, 12 mm

▌ 3 long tube beads

▌ 3 seed beads

▌ Beading needle

▌ Beading thread

Instructions

1. Enlarge the pattern on page 116 to the size indicated. Trace two hearts from the pattern onto the pieces of mat board, and cut them out with the craft knife.

2. Round off the corners of the 5-inch-square (12.5 cm) piece of felt.

3. If using a home scanner and ink-jet printer to transfer your photo, size it to fit within the boundaries of the heart pattern, then transfer it onto the transfer film. Iron the photo onto the cream or white felt. Trim the edges of the transferred image and set it aside.

4. With the sewing needle and beading thread, hand sew a line of ¼-inch-long (6 mm) gathering stitches around the edges of the 5-inch-square (12.5 cm) piece of felt. Pull up slightly, and insert a small handful of fiberfill.

5. Lay one of the mat board hearts inside the pouch that you've created out of felt and fiberfill. Pull up the gathers, and add more fiberfill as needed to make a puffy heart. Tighten the gathers at the back of the heart. Take a few stitches across the back in several directions, joining the sides of the gathered felt. Secure with a knot and tie off. Trim the thread.

6. Smear a little glue on the back of the trimmed felt photo, and position it on the front of the heart. Allow it to dry.

7. With the embroidery needle and pearl cotton thread, use a blanket stitch or other decorative stitch to tack down the edges of the photo. Keep the stitches small and near the edges.

8. Decorate the heart with embroidery stitches, beads, and fringe as desired (see the next column for fringe instructions).

9. Glue the second mat heart to the back of the pin, covering all the raw edges. Weight the pin down by placing a book on top of it until the glue is dry.

10. Glue the pin back high on the back of the heart.

Instructions for Beaded Fringe

If you want to add beaded fringe and a tassel to your heart, you'll begin by attaching each dangle separately. Thread a needle with beading thread and knot it. Take a small stitch in the heart fabric, close to and behind the lower edge of the heart. Pick up three pearl seed beads and a gold seed bead on the needle, and slide them up to the felt. Pick up a long tube bead, a 10mm (⅜ in) round bead, and one more seed bead. Bring the thread around the last seed bead, and push the needle back through all of the beads to the felt, near the point where you began. Take a small stitch or two to secure the thread well before trimming it. Add three more dangles about ¼-inch (6 mm) apart. Add four strands on the other side of the heart in the same position. Within the space that you've left blank at the point of the heart, add a beaded tassel. Begin by pulling knotted beading thread through the tip of the heart from the back. Slide on an 8 mm (⁵⁄₁₆ in) round bead, then a 12mm (½ in) round bead, followed by a tube and a seed bead. Push the needle and thread back up through all the beads, and secure to the felt. Add two more strands through the original 8 mm (⁵⁄₁₆ in) round bead in the same manner.

Treasure Box

S This luxurious box for jewelry, buttons, coins, or charms has the soft touch of felt.

DESIGNED BY
NANCY WORRELL

You Will Need

▐ 1 piece of embossed, maroon felt, about 1 foot (30 cm) square
▐ 1 piece of black felt, about 1 foot (30 cm) square
▐ 1 piece of plastic canvas, about 1 foot (30 cm) square
▐ Skein of #5 black pearl cotton thread
▐ Black sewing thread
▐ Black, flat, corded braid, ½ yard (45 cm)
▐ Black and silver decorative button, ¾ inch (1.9 cm) wide
▐ Black trim tassel, 1½ inches (3.8 cm) long
▐ Scissors
▐ Chenille needle
▐ Sewing needle

Instructions

1. To form the bottom of the box, cut out a rectangle of maroon felt, black felt, and plastic canvas that each measure 3 x 4 inches (7.5 x 10 cm). Cut the long sides of the box from two pieces of maroon felt, black felt, and plastic canvas that each measure 2 x 4 inches (5 x 10 cm). Cut the short sides of the box from two pieces of maroon felt, black felt, and plastic canvas that each measure 2 x 3 inches (5 x 7.5 cm). Cut the top of the box out of one piece of maroon felt and one piece of black felt that each measure 4 x 5 inches

(10 x 12.5 cm). To make the top sides of the box, cut out two circles, each measuring 3 inches (7.5 cm) in diameter from maroon felt, black felt, and plastic. Cut each piece in half to form two identical semicircular pieces. To make the top flap, cut out a triangle of felt from one piece of maroon and one piece of black felt, each measuring 4 inches (10 cm) at the base and 2¼ (5.6 cm) inches on the sides.

2. Sandwich the plastic between the pieces of maroon and black felt that you've cut for the bottom and the long, short, and top sides of the box. Place the embossed side of the maroon felt face-up, so that the back is facing the plastic. Use the chenille needle and pearl cotton thread to blanket-stitch (see page 114) around the edge of each sandwiched piece.

3. Place the maroon and black felt pieces for the top together with the embossed side of the maroon felt face-up. Do the same for the top flap pieces. Blanket-stitch the edges.

4. To assemble the box, begin by aligning one bottom piece and one side piece with the maroon sides together. Thread the chenille needle with the black pearl cotton thread, and lace the side to the bottom through the blanket stitching. Knot the thread at the end of the line of lacing, and clip it. Add the three other side pieces to the bottom in the same manner, configuring them as shown at the right.

5. To form the box, fold two of the side pieces up with the maroon felt facing outward. Lace them together through the blanket stitching as you did in step 4. Continue to lace the sides up until a box is formed.

6. To form the box's top or lid, begin at one corner of the top side, or half-circular piece, and lace the top piece along the curve with the maroon felt facing outwards. (You'll create a roof-like curve when you do this.) Repeat this process to lace up the other side of the lid. Lace the triangular flap to the bottom edge of the lid's front.

7. To attach the lid, position it on the box. Lace across the back side to form a hinge.

8. Thread the sewing needle with a length of black thread. To add the decorative braid to the box's lid, turn one end of the braid under into a circular configuration, and tack it in place with thread to form a medallion. Place the circular medallion on the point of the triangular flap, and tack it in place. Tack the braid up and over the top of the box and down to the base, leaving space to add another line of braid beside it. Turn the braid in a U-shape at the base, and bring it back over the lid until it meets the medallion. Tuck the ends of the braid under the medallion, and tack them down. Trim the ends as needed.

9. Stitch the tassel onto the medallion. Tack the button in place on top of it.

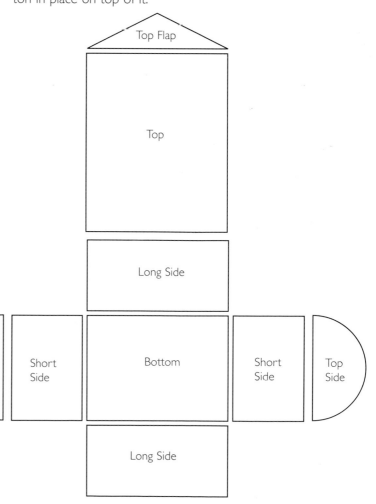

Great Grandmother's Moonlit Path Quilt

This quilt-like design, based on the traditional log cabin pattern, was inspired by a box of old costume jewelry belonging to the designer.

The moon, one of my mother's old jewelry pieces, shines down on a white path of leaves nestled in a magic garden of flowers. The path leads you to great grandma's house behind the garden gate....

When I look at this piece, I can almost smell those rare evenings when the garden was so sweet on the breeze. I would gaze out the open window, next to her bed piled high with quilts, and watch the flowers and fireflies till I fell asleep.

DESIGNED BY
BILLI R. S. ROTHOVE

You Will Need

- Plain felt backing in color of your choice, 21 × 50 inches (52.5 × 125 cm)
- Strips of embossed and plain felts in colors of your choice to be cut to fit sides of piece
- Old costume jewelry or other found objects
- Fabric or craft glue
- Rotary cutter with straight blade
- Self-healing cutting mat
- 18-inch (45 cm) steel ruler
- Scissors
- Embroidery floss in color of your choice
- Embroidery needle
- Thimble
- ⅜ × 21-inch (9 mm × 52.5 cm) wooden dowel
- 2 screw eyes
- Small wire cutters (optional)
- Sewing machine

Instructions

1. Referring to the figure at right, cut a piece of felt that measures 10½ inches (26.3 × 26.3 cm) square for the center of the quilt. Fold the plain felt backing in half so that it measures 21 by 25 inches (52.5 × 62.5 cm). Place the center square 8 inches (20 cm) down from the top of the fold in the backing (which will form the sleeve), and 6 inches (15 cm) from the bottom.

2. Use the rotary cutter, mat, and steel ruler to cut two contrasting strips of felt that measure 1½ inches (3.75 cm) wide by 10½ inches (26.3 cm) long. Place them along the top and bottom edges of the square.

3. Cut and add two more strips that border the sides of the square and the strips that you've just placed. Continue to add pieces of felt in this fashion until you reach the edge of

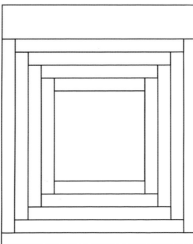

the felt base at the bottom, and leave a 2-inch (5 cm) sleeve at the top.

4. Choose from the pieces of costume jewelry, buttons, or other objects that you'd like to use on top of the quilt. Play with a design by moving the pieces around. If needed, use wire cutters to trim pieces of jewelry. (When this designer moved her pieces around, she found that she wanted to hint at an abstracted path and mountain scene with the pieces that she had saved from her grandmother's jewelry box.)

5. Remove the jewelry pieces, then cut and add felt pieces within the center square to serve as a background for the jewelry pieces.

6. Once all of the felt pieces are laid out, and you're satisfied with your composition, begin gluing each of them in place one by one on the felt base.

7. After gluing down the felt strips and pieces of your design, reposition the pieces of jewelry and other objects. Apply heavy glue to the back of each piece and press it in place on the quilt. (Be aware of the weight of each of the pieces you're applying, and use an appropriate amount of glue.) Allow the piece to dry overnight on a flat surface.

8. To lend the quilt a handmade look, use embroidery thread to add cross-stitches (see page 114) on top of several joining seams of the quilt.

9. Cut the dowel rod to fit the width of the piece, or 21 inches (52.5 cm). Add a screw eye on either end of the rod, and slide it into place. Your quilt is now ready for hanging.

Celtic Banner

T This Celtic cross is based on one found in Ireland at Montasterboice, dating from the early times of Christianity.

DESIGNED BY
KAREN M. BENNETT

You Will Need

- 1½ yards (3.8 cm) of brown plush felt, cut to a piece that is 30 × 50 inches (75 × 12.5 cm)
- 20 × 36-inch (50 × 90 cm) of piece moss green plush felt
- Large roll of tracing paper
- Woodburning tool with small, rounded point and shading point
- Protective mask to prevent inhaling fumes
- Straight pins
- Fabric scissors
- Sewing machine
- Size 15 needle
- Thread
- Overhead projector (optional)

Note: The following are a couple of ways to deal with enlarging a pattern of the size of the cross that you see in this banner:

*If you have an overhead projector available, it provides an easy way to enlarge a pattern such as this cross. To do this, tape large pieces of tracing paper onto a blank wall big enough to hold your enlarged pattern. Place the pattern on the overhead projector, and project it onto the tracing paper. Draw over the lines of the design with a black marker.

*If you aren't able to use a projector, you can enlarge the image one portion at a time on a copy machine, then piece them all together before tracing the outline of the design onto a large piece of tracing paper.

Instructions

1. Enlarge the pattern on page 123 to the size indicated. Pin the paper pattern to the brown felt. Place the felt on a table outside or in a very well-ventilated room. Put on the protective mask. Plug in the woodburner equipped with a small, rounded point. With the paper still attached, begin by burning the outlines of the design. Use a very light touch with the woodburner. The paper and felt will burn and melt quickly, so be careful not to burn through to the other side of it.

2. After you've completed this part, allow the woodburner to cool and insert a shading point (shaped like a flat shovel). Burn the recessed, background areas of the design.

3. Once the design is burned, cut out the cross with scissors.

4. Trim the brown felt to a piece that measures 30 × 50 inches (75 × 125 cm). Beginning on one of the long sides of the piece, turn under a 1-inch (2.5 cm) hem. Miter each of the corners by turning them under at a diagonal. Pin the hem in place with straight pins, and sew it up with a ½-inch (1.3 cm) seam. Repeat for the bottom of the banner and the other side.

5. To form the banner's sleeve, turn under the top edge 3 inches (7.5 cm), and sew it in place with a ½-inch (1.3 cm) seam.

6. Place the cross on the right side of the brown felt and center it. Pin it in place before sewing around the edges with a size 15 needle.

Felt Tree Skirt

This gloriously gorgeous tree skirt will dazzle even the most sophisticated eyes. It's all put together with fabric glue and hand stitching, and, although it takes time, the results are well worth the effort.

DESIGNED BY
KIM TIBBALS-THOMPSON

You Will Need

- Roll of brown kraft paper
- 3 yards (2.7 m) ivory plush felt,
  54 inches (1.4 m) wide
- 1½ yards (1.4 m) taupe plush felt,
  54 inches (1.4 m) wide
- 2 yards (1.8 m) dark green plush felt,
  54 inches (1.4 m) wide
- 2 yards (1.8 m) blue plush felt,
  54 inches (1.4 m) wide
- 25 yards (22.5 m) 1 mm tan
  "rat tail" silk cord
- 60 yards (54 m)of 1mm blue-gray "rat tail" silk cord
- 2 yards (1.8 m) of green, twisted drapery cord,
  1½ inches (3.8 cm) thick
- 6-inch (15 cm) strip of hook-and-eye fastener
- Hot glue gun
- Awl
- Yardstick
- Straight pins
- Vanishing ink fabric marker
- Large curved needle with eye large
  enough
  for silk cord
- 2-inch (5 cm) strip of hook-and-
  loop tape

Instructions

1. Fold the ivory plush felt in half,
wrong sides together, to make a
54- inch (1.4 m) square. Cut along
the fold to create two 54-inch-
square (1.4 m) pieces.

2. Fold each of the squares in half.
Place a yardstick along one of the
folded lines, and find the point that lies
27 inches (67.5 cm) from the edge, or
the center point of the square. Mark it
with a straight pin. Open the square out,

and pivot the yardstick around this center point. Mark
at intervals with pins as you go. Cut the piece into a
54-inch (1.4 m) diameter ivory circle of felt. Repeat
this process to cut another circle.

3. Place the circles wrong sides together. Cut an
identical line through both thicknesses that runs from
the edge to the center of the circle. To accommodate
the tree, cut away circular pieces from the center that
are approximately 7 inches (9.5 cm) in diameter. Set
one of the halves of the skirt aside.

4. Lay the skirt on top of the taupe felt, and use the
vanishing ink marker to trace half of its circumference.
Use the diagram on this page as a guide to trace a
curved line within this semicircular area. Cut out a single thickness

of taupe felt along this line to form a decorative over-lay for the skirt.

5. Lightly trace the curved edge of the taupe felt onto the circular skirt with a vanishing ink marker. Remove the taupe piece, and trim the skirt to 1 inch (2.5 cm) inside of the line you've drawn (toward the skirt's edge). This will allow enough room to overlap the taupe piece on the skirt.

6. Use the hot glue gun to run a line of glue along the curved line that you cut on the skirt. Overlap the taupe piece, making sure that it matches the edges of the skirt, and glue it in place.

7. Place the front and back of the skirt together with the right sides out and the wrong sides together. Match all edges of the skirt including the slit and opening. About 2 inches (5 cm) inside all of the edges

except the center opening, tack the back and front together with glue.

8. Position the green twisted drapery cord to form a vine on the top surface of the skirt, hiding the seam between the taupe overlay and the skirt. Tuck in one raw edge in the center between the front and back of the skirt. Glue the vine into place.

9. To make the leaves, enlarge the leaf patterns on page 126 to the size indicated, and cut one set out of heavy paper. Before cutting any leaves out of felt, lay out these paper patterns on top of the skirt in a placement that mimics our finished piece, or a configuration of your own. Once you've decided on placement, cut a front and a back for each leaf out of plush felt, making one side dark green and the other blue. Match the two sides of each leaf, and lightly tack them together with hot glue. Position them on the skirt as you create each one.

10. Use the patterns to cut the olives out of double thicknesses of taupe and green felt. With wrong sides together, lightly tack the pieces together with hot glue, and place them on the skirt.

11. After you've made all the components and placed them, trace lightly with the vanishing ink marker around all of your pieces so that you can reposition them later. To make it even clearer, write a number on the back of each leaf or olive and a corresponding number on the skirt. Remove the leaves and olives from the skirt.

12. Thread your needle with blue-gray silk cord, and use a long stitch that is about ½ inch (1.3 cm) long and ½ inch (1.3 cm) apart on the edges of all the leaves. (Use the awl to punch holes through the felt to accommodate the needle.) Edge the olives in tan silk cord.

13. At each point that a leaf joins or emerges from the vine of drapery cord, sew and wrap each junction with six loops of blue-gray rat tail, knotting and trimming the ends on the back side of the vine/drapery cord.

14. Liberally hot glue the leaves and olives in place. Position the skirt so that the slit is closed, and the large leaf overlaps the seam. Pull back the leaf, and hot glue the strip of hook-and-loop tape to it. Then attach the other side of the hook-and-loop tape where it falls on the face of the skirt, so that you can use this strip as a closure.

15. To finish the skirt, hand stitch along the entire outer edge of the skirt, the opening seam, and the inner circle as you did for the leaves and olives.

The following pages contain a gallery of unusual works in felt that range from an exquisite handmade felt rug to a vibrant hooked rug created from commericially-made strips of felt.

Although this book does not explore how to make your own felt, we thought you'd enjoy seeing some beautiful things created by artists who make and dye their own felt before shaping or molding it into a finished piece of their own design. Other pieces in this gallery show you the imaginative heights that can be reached by designers who use commercially-made felt.

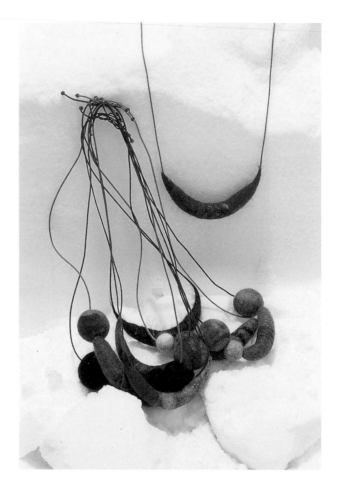

Left to right:

Jean Hicks (Seattle, Washington), *Ziggurat,* Handmade felt hat made from merino wool shaped by hand.

Jorie Johnson (Kyoto, Japan), *A Touch of Colour,* Pendants of handmade wool felt with glass beads and cord. Photo by K. Nishimura.

Dale Liles (Knoxville, Tennessee), Handmade felt purse.

Beatriz Schaaf-Giesser (Winnenden, Germany), Industrial felt carpet with cut out areas of shag carpet.

Jorie Johnson (Kyoto, Japan), *Melting Rainbow*, Handmade felt carpet. Photo by K. Nishimura.

Nora Flatley (Seattle, Washington), *Airplane Dress*, Hand sewn commercial felt dress with embroidery thread and sculpted wool.

Left to right:

Ewa Kuniczak (Kincardine-on-Forth, Scotland), *Cacti Hats*, Seamless handmade felt made from hand-dyed merino wool, hand-molded.

Barbara Carleton Evans (Ventura, California), *Sunday Afternoon Drive*, Felt doll embellished with appliquéd ribbons and embroidery.

Vivian Peritts (Marietta, Georgia), *Chicken Rug*, Hooked felt rug.

Nora Flatley (Seattle, Washington), *Wedding Dress with Accessories*, Hand sewn commercial felt dress with embroidery thread, sculpted wool, and glitter.

Salley Mavor (Falmouth, Massachusetts), *The Pink House,* Appliquéd wool felt and found objects appliqué

Salley Mavor (Falmouth, Massachusetts), *The Storyteller*, Velveteen, wool felt, found objects, wire.

Top to bottom:

Barbara Carleton Evans (Ventura, California), *Earth Goddess,* Felt pin embellished with embroidery and beads.

Barbara Carleton Evans (Ventura, California), *Akua's Child,* Felt doll embellished with African trade beads and embroidery.

Connie Matricardi (Baltimore, Maryland), *William Shakespeare and James Joyce Pillows,* Assembled, sewn, and stuffed pillows.

Embroidery Stitch Guide

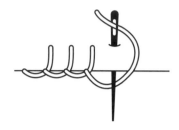

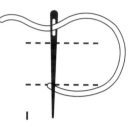

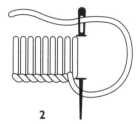

Blanket Stitch

To edge felt with a standard-sized blanket stitch, come up through the felt with your needle about ¼ inch (.6 cm) in from the edge. Hold the thread lightly with your thumb, and go back through the fabric, bringing the needle over the thread. Pull the stitch into place.

Buttonhole Stitch

This stitch makes a great edging. Make closely placed loops with your needle, placing the thread underneath the needle each time you make one. Notice that this stitch uses the same technique as the blanket stitch, but places the stitches closer together.

Chain Stitch

To make a pretty chain stitch, pull your needle up through the felt and loop the thread underneath the needle before pulling it through.

Cross Stitch

To sew decorative cross stitches, make parallel straight stitches, as shown, and follow with reverse parallel straight stitches to create crosses.

Fly Stitch

To create a fly stitch with ribbon, bring the needle up at A, down at B, up at C (catching the ribbon with your needle as you bring it through), then down at D.

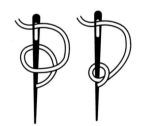

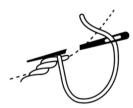

French Knot

To make French knots, bring your needle up through the felt, wrap the thread once or twice around the needle, and hold it against the face of the felt with your thumb to create slight tension. Flatten the needle against the felt's surface, and insert it close to the starting point before pulling the needle through to the other side.

Stem Stitch

To create a line with stem stitches, use your needle to make diagonally-placed stitches of equal size that follow a line.

Straight Stitch

To make simple straight stitches with thread or ribbon, bring the needle up through the felt, and pull it back through the felt at a point far enough away to create the length of stitch that you desire.

Patterns

PLAYING CARD COASTERS, page 12

(Enlarge all 185%)

STAR PILLOW, page 24

(Enlarge 400%)

FLOWER PILLOW, page 88

Petal Unit

(Enlarge 400%)

Leaf

BUTTERFLY PIN, page 34

Wing

Wing

(Enlarge 200%)

Back body

Front body

AFTERNOON SKETCH BOOK, page 21

(Enlarge 340%)

FOLK ART BANNER, page 26

Top

A-(Repeating Stripe)

Bottom

(Enlarge 250%)

C

B

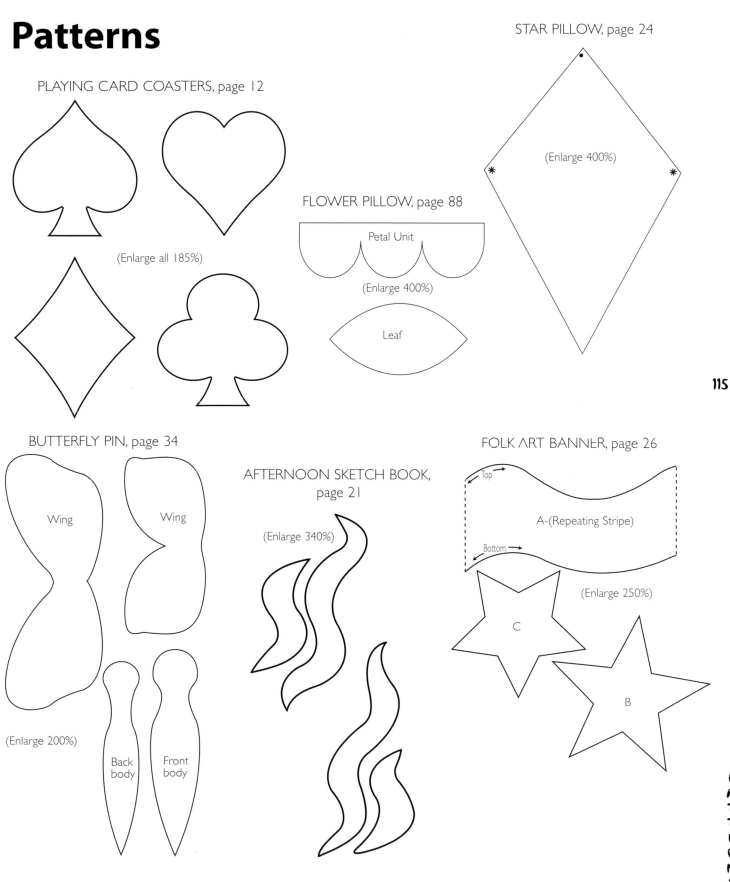

MOSAIC FRAME,
page 20

COLORFUL STITCHED
STRING PURSE, page 46

SPLASHY MARTINI SKIRT, page 48

(Enlarge 400%)

Front flap

(fold line)

Back

(Enlarge 400%)

Front
(Enlarge 400%)

116

(Enlarge 335%)

HEART PIN, page 94

(Enlarge 180%)

SOFT 'N CLASSY HATS, page 42

(Enlarge 650%)

Brim

Stand

Crown

REVERSE APPLIQUÉ VEST, page 44

(Enlarge 250%)

Make three
copies of
pattern

MARINE FLAG WALL BANNER,
page 22 (Enlarge 400%)

Note: Colors of felt are indicated as follows: white (W), blue (B), black (BL), red (R), yellow (Y). Letters of marine alphabet are indicated above each square.

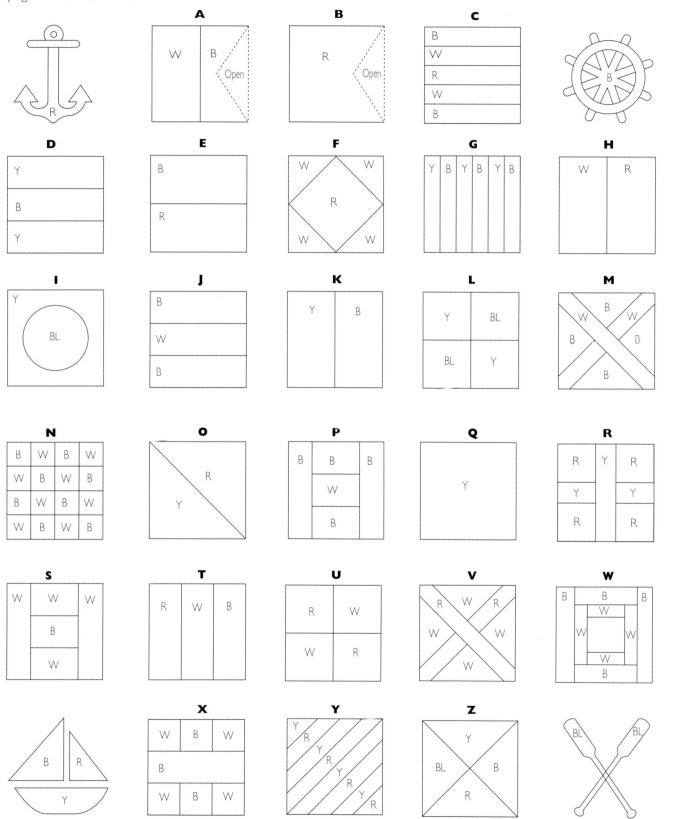

117

RABBIT IN A HAT, page 56

(Enlarge 360%)

Back of head
cut 1

Front of head
cut 1

Ear
cut 2

Arm
cut 2

Top   Top

cut slit

(Enlarge 360%)

Body
cut 1

MOON AND STARS WINDOW VALANCE, page 52

cut 3

cut 1

(Enlarge 345%)

cut 6

cut 2

(Enlarge 290%)

118

TABLE RUNNER,
page 86

EMBROIDERY BOX, page 93

(Enlarge 180%)

(Enlarge 425%)

Border design

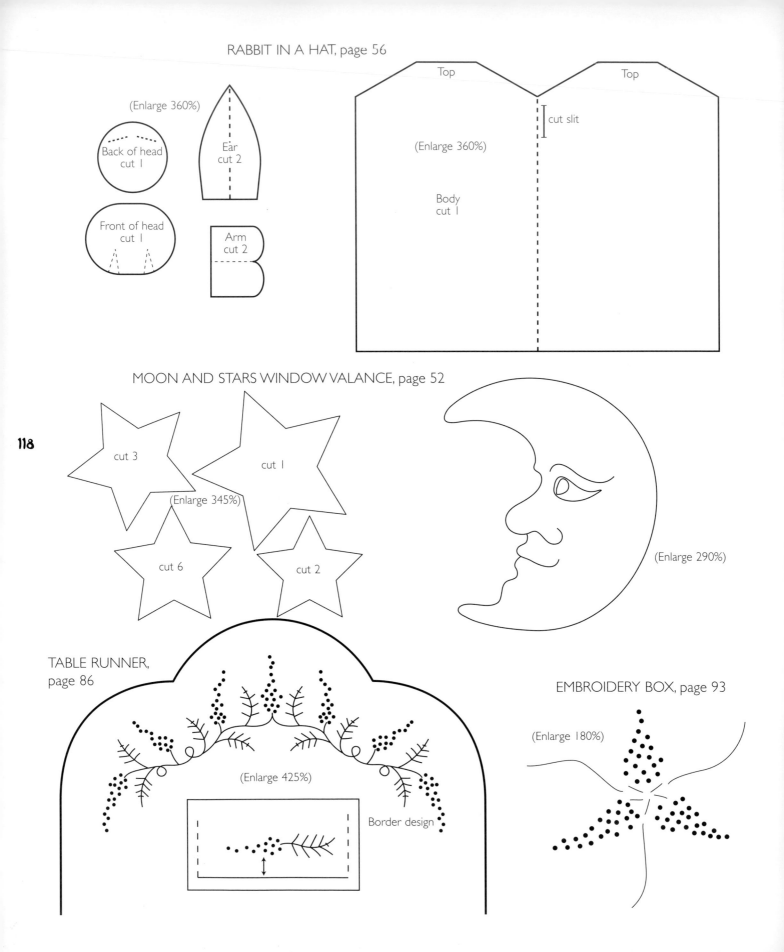

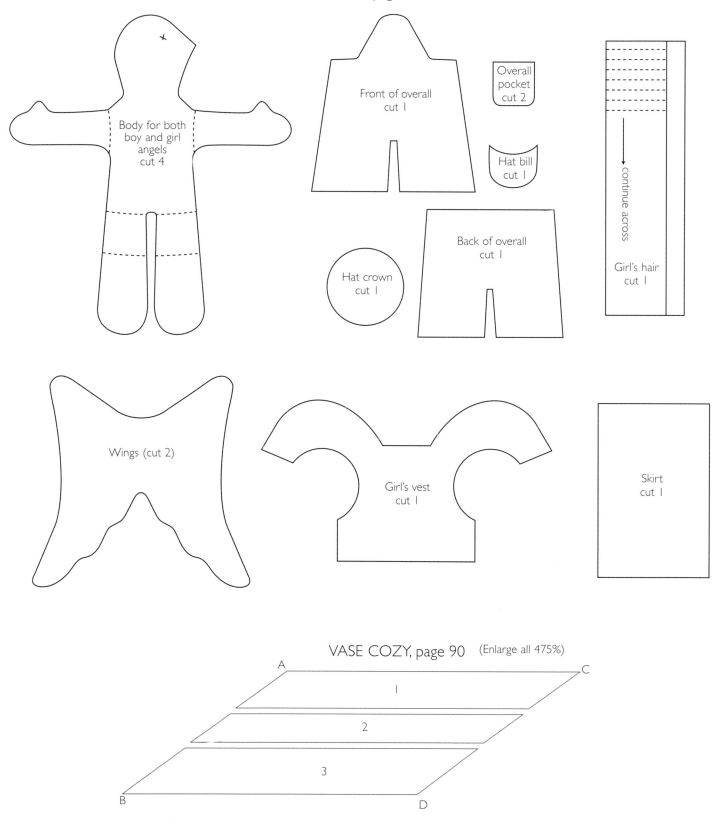

HOE DOWN ANGELS, page 54 (Enlarge all 285%)

Body for both
boy and girl
angels
cut 4

Front of overall
cut 1

Overall
pocket
cut 2

Hat bill
cut 1

Back of overall
cut 1

Hat crown
cut 1

continue across

Girl's hair
cut 1

Wings (cut 2)

Girl's vest
cut 1

Skirt
cut 1

VASE COZY, page 90 (Enlarge all 475%)

A

C

1

2

3

B

D

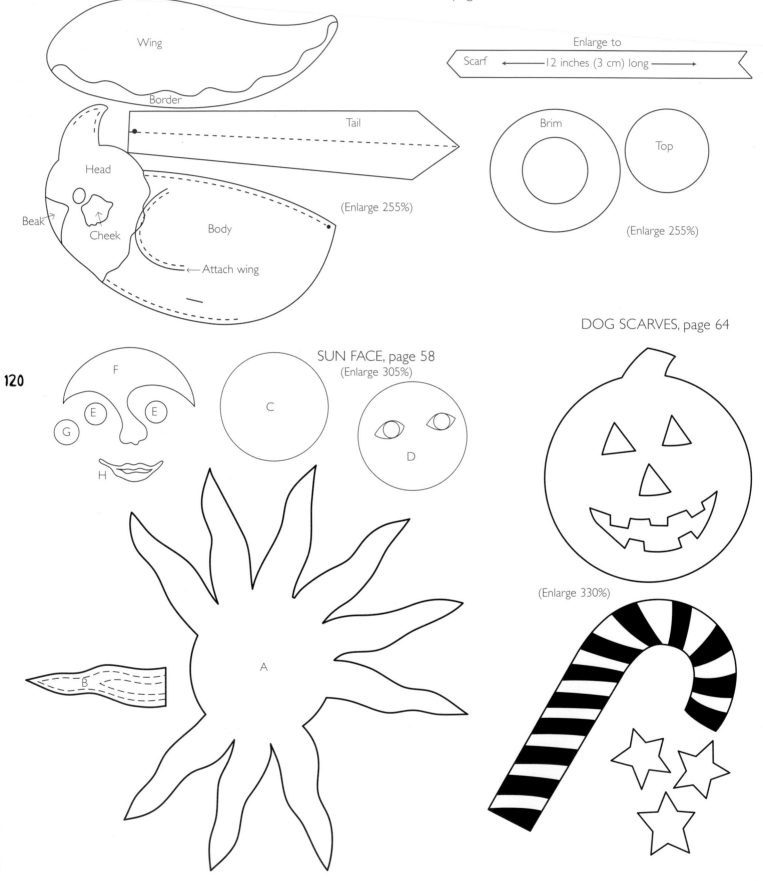

COCKATIELS, page 50

Wing

Border

Enlarge to

Scarf ← 12 inches (3 cm) long →

Tail

Head

Brim

Top

Beak

Cheek

Body

← Attach wing

(Enlarge 255%)

(Enlarge 255%)

DOG SCARVES, page 64

120

F

SUN FACE, page 58
(Enlarge 305%)

E   E

G

C

D

H

(Enlarge 330%)

A

B

PET MOBILE, page 62 (Enlarge 200%)

121

CAT MAT, page 66
(Enlarge 225%)

Tail
cut 1

Head
cut 1

Paws
cut 2

C
cut 2

A
cut 2

D
Cat tail

B
cut 1

Add ¼ inch (6 mm) seam
allowance to A, B, C

E

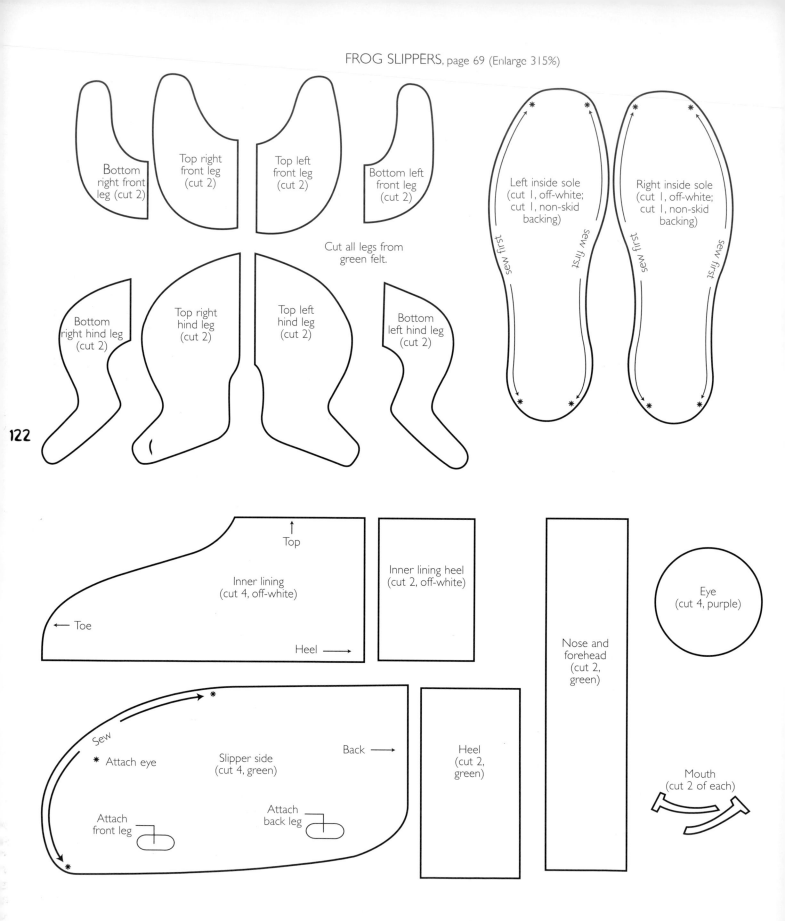

Bottom right front leg (cut 2)

Top right front leg (cut 2)

Top left front leg (cut 2)

Bottom left front leg (cut 2)

Cut all legs from green felt.

Left inside sole (cut 1, off-white; cut 1, non-skid backing)

sew first

Right inside sole (cut 1, off-white; cut 1, non-skid backing)

sew first

Bottom right hind leg (cut 2)

Top right hind leg (cut 2)

Top left hind leg (cut 2)

Bottom left hind leg (cut 2)

122

Top

Inner lining (cut 4, off-white)

← Toe

Heel →

Inner lining heel (cut 2, off-white)

Nose and forehead (cut 2, green)

Eye (cut 4, purple)

Sew

* Attach eye

Slipper side (cut 4, green)

Back →

Attach front leg

Attach back leg

Heel (cut 2, green)

Mouth (cut 2 of each)

STOCKING,
page 71
(Enlarge 510%)

cut 2

CELTIC BANNER, page 100 (Enlarge 450%)

123

EMBROIDERED PLACEMATS AND NAPKIN RINGS,
page 82

(Enlarge 230%)

A

B

MOSAIC FELT BOTTLE, page 84

X

Flowers

(Enlarge 250%)

Leaves

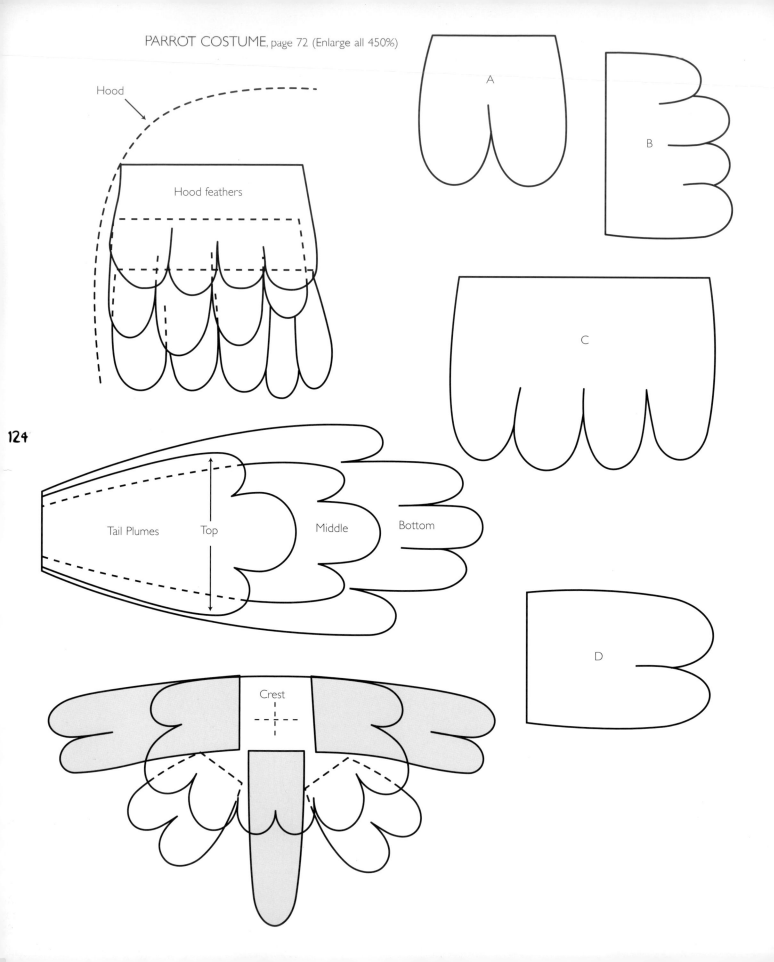

Hood

Hood feathers

A

B

C

D

124

Tail Plumes

Top

Middle

Bottom

Crest

PARROT COSTUME, page 72

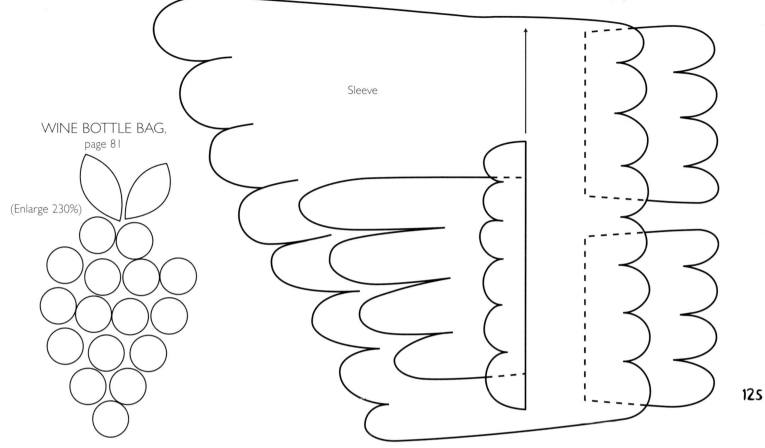

WINE BOTTLE BAG,
page 81

(Enlarge 230%)

Sleeve

125

DAFFODIL PLANT POKES, page 74

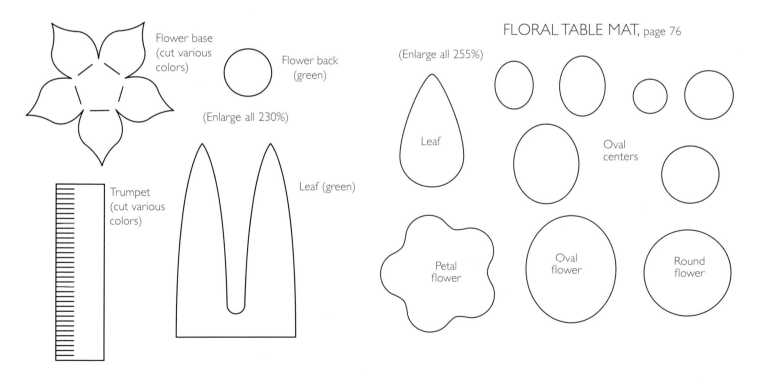

Flower base
(cut various
colors)

Flower back
(green)

(Enlarge all 230%)

Trumpet
(cut various
colors)

Leaf (green)

FLORAL TABLE MAT, page 76

(Enlarge all 255%)

Leaf

Oval
centers

Petal
flower

Oval
flower

Round
flower

PATTERNS

126

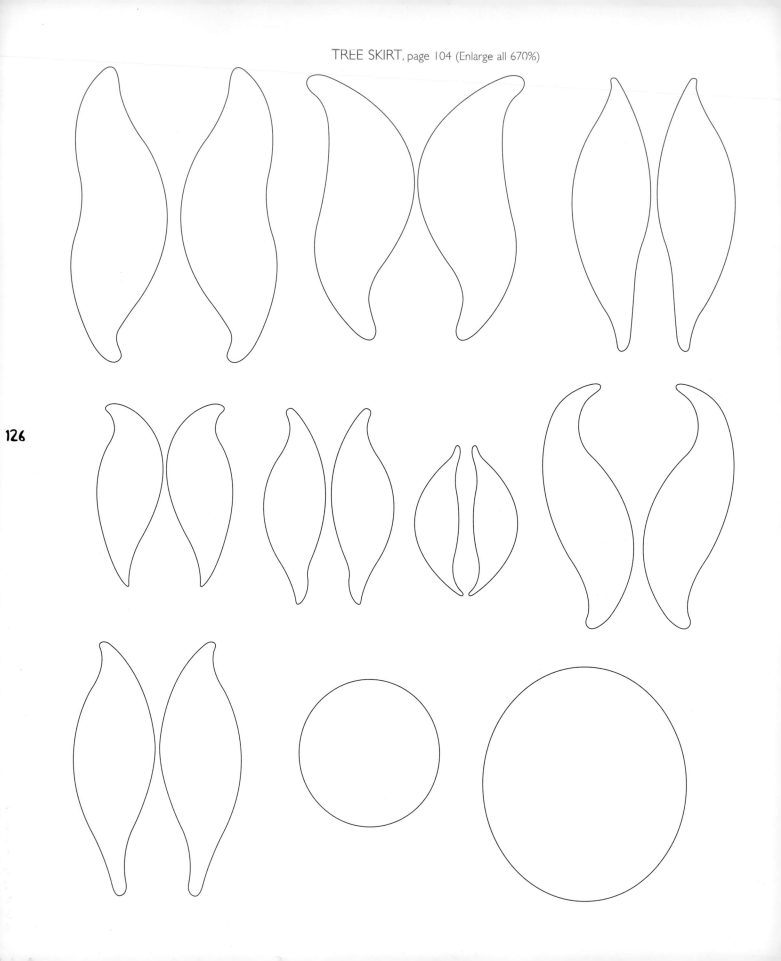

DESIGNERS

TERRY ALBRIGHT is a freelance designer who works in silk embroidery, felt crafts, and glass blowing. Several of her designs have been published. She makes her home in Westville, New Jersey, with her husband Tom and son Dylan.

BETTY AUTH of Houston, Texas, is well-known in the crafts field as an author and teacher. Through many features in publications such as *Arts and Crafts Magazine* (Krause Publications) and *Decorative Woodcrafts* (Better Homes and Gardens), she has helped spark renewed interest in the craft of woodburning. More than 150 of her craft designs have been published in national magazines, and she has made several television appearances including those on Lifetime's *Our Home* and HGTV's *Carol Duvall Show*.

KAREN M. BENNETT has been a member of the Southern Highland Craft Guild since 1983. She teaches tatting, sewing, and needle arts, as well as selling her work to galleries. Her work has been featured in several of Lark's other books.

TANA BOERGER is an entrepreneur and classically trained artist who lives in Washington, D.C. Her works on canvas hang in collections in Europe and North America, and her painted furniture graces fine homes throughout the United States.

BARBARA BRUNSON has been creating soft craft projects for the past several years. She says that she is continually torn between her love for the drawing table, the sewing machine, and her backyard. She lives in Hillsboro, Oregon, with her husband and two daughters.

MARY D'ALTON of Spring Green, Wisconsin, is a photostylist and propmaker who holds a degree in costume design. She uses her sewing skills and expert design sense in a variety of creative endeavors, especially those that feature fine ribbon and buttons. She is the author of *The Christmas Stocking Book* published by Lark Books.

HOLLY DECKER is a banker who lives in Asheville, North Carolina, and enjoys creating decorative costumes for dogs in her spare time.

BARBARA EVANS has worked as a designer for craft magazines for 20 years. Her work has been published in craft and doll magazines and some bead and doll books.

MARGARET GREGG, of Limestone, Tennessee, paints and sculpts in addition to working in fiber. Her studio, located in an historic grist mill, supplies much of her inspiration.

DANA IRWIN, who lives in Asheville, North Carolina, is a multimedia artist. She says that the last time she worked with felt was at age seven when she made a pin holder project in Brownie Scouts.

MAGGIE D. JONES has a secret ambition to spend the rest of her life discovering hidden treasures in boxes stored in dusty attics across the country. Meanwhile, she teaches art and photography to high school students in Greer, South Carolina. She has always made things with her hands and is a published photographer.

GAY D. FAY KELLY of Austin, Texas, has worn many hats in her life, but most have some connection to her degree in art and art history from Rice University. Her immediate family includes—at last count— a husband, two daughters, a dog, a cat, a guinea pig, a gerbil, a mouse, and a parakeet.

MONA-KATRI MAKELA, who lives in the mountains of New Mexico, was a student at the Rudolph Steiner School in Helsinki, Finland, from kindergarten on. The experience provided her with an appreciation of art and expression. She enjoys designing and making art with a variety of media.

CHRIS MALONE lives on the beautiful southern Oregon coast. A member of the Society of Craft Designers, she has had many designs published in magazines and books. She loves all kinds of needlework, but has a special fondness for working with felt.

BARBARA MATTHIESSEN lives in Washington State with her husband and, as she puts it, several extremely spoiled dogs and cats. Working with felt and combining it with other mediums is one of her favorite creative outlets.

VIVIAN PERITTS is a freelance designer who works with manufacturers who are developing craft products. She is an author and frequent guest on television craft and decorating shows.

BILLI R. S. ROTHOVE, a Tennessee fiber artist, has been creating expressive images in fibers and needleart for 25 years. She began weaving at the Kansas City Art Instititute, where she earned a BFA in fiber, and has continued to earn graduate and postgradute degrees in her field as a studio artist and educator.

PAT G. SAMUELS is a studio textile artist whose improvisational designs combine appliqué, hand and machine stitching, painting, and drawing to create unique layered fabrics that are used in a variety of applications. She lives and works in the Blue Ridge Mountains of North Carolina.

DEBBIE SCHMITZ has been designing from her home in LeMars, Iowa, for over ten years. She specializes in designs for felt and fabric as well as dolls. Her designs are quick and easy to fit her busy life with her husband and four children.

BRENDA STAR uses color and form to express the human spirit's connection to nature and its healing effects. Her painting and clay studios are located in DeLand, Florida. You can see more of her work at her website, www.emanations.com.

ROSE SZABO lives in Weaverville, North Carolina, and is a public school art teacher. She enjoys designing on her computer and translating her ideas into sculptural pieces made of clay and fabric. She owns a variety of pet birds that inspire her work. You can see more of her work at www.darling.home.mindspring.com.

TERRY TAYLOR lends his creative spirit full-time to Lark Books, and, in his spare time, glues, pastes, and otherwise assembles works of art using a wide range of media from old CDs to broken china. His work has been exhibited in galleries, and his designs have been featured in numerous publications.

KIM TIBBALS-THOMPSON resides in Waynesville, North Carolina. She is a frequent contributor to craft books and enjoys drawing, sewing, gardening, herbal crafting and broom making. By day, she is a graphic designer.

KAREN TIMM, who lives in Madison, Wisconsin, is the owner of Books About You, a company that "creates handmade blank books to fill with life's adventures." She loves to work with fabrics to make useful objects.

DEE DEE TRIPLET, who lives in the Great Smokey Mountains of North Carolina, is a cloth dollmaker and teacher. She is totally enamored with fabric and anything creative and can't understand how anyone can ever be bored.

NICOLE TUGGLE uses a variety of paper craft techniques to create unique cards and gift items. She uses her art as a means of communication, emotional release, and as a celebration of the simple act of giving. She currently resides in Asheville, North Carolina, where she is waiting for her true passion to fall from the sky and bonk her on the head!

LISA VIVEIROS lives in Northhampton, Massachusetts, with her husband and two children. She holds a degree in interior design, and designs projects for National Nonwovens, using their line of wool felt.

CAROLYNN WILLIAMS designs silk embroidery projects, quilts, and felt projects. She has had many designs published and does custom sewing for clients. She lives in southern New Jersey with her husband Vince. Her daughter, Terry Albright, is also featured in this book.

NANCY WORRELL is an author and designer who has published more than 100 articles. She has authored two books entitled *Paper Plus: Unique Projects Using Handmade Paper* (Krause Publications) and *Beautiful Wedding Crafts* (Lark Books). To see more of her work, visit her website at http://hometown.aol.com/designs by Nancy Worrell.

ELLEN ZAHOREC is a mixed media artist who works out of her Cincinatti, Ohio, studio. She specializes in works incorporating handmade paper and collage. Her work has been exhibited internationally and is included in many private and corporate collections.

SUPPLIERS

Embossed felts, plush felts, colored felts:
Kunin Felt
United States and Canada:
P.O. Box 5000
Hampton, NH 03843-5000
800-292-7900
fax: 603-929-6180
Europe:
Foss S.A.R.C.
Z.I Compans
Rue Henri Becquerel
Mitry Mory, France
331-602-10303
Australia:
Foss Australasia
A.C.N. 005 852 380
14-16 Hardner Rd.
MT Waverley
Victoria, 3149 Australia
61-395435533
www.kuninfelt.com

Wool felt:
National Nonwovens
P.O. Box 150
Easthampton, MA 01027
To find out the name of a retailer nearest you,
call 800-333-3469
fax: 413-527-0456
www.nationalnonwovens.com

Speciality items:
Hand-dyed variegated silk ribbon for project on p. 86:
Heirlooms Silk Bouquet
from "La Coleccion de Colores" by Elouise Gomez
504 Roxbury Dr.
Safety Harbor, FL 34695
727-669-88807

Hand-dyed pearl cotton thread for projects on
pps. 44 and 46:
Artfabrik
324 Vincent Place
Elgin, IL 60123
847-931-7684

Cardboard furniture for project on p. 91:
Mixed Nuts
221 Rayon Drive
Old Hickory, TN 37138
615-847-3889
www.kraftables.com

INDEX